A Marriage Built To Last

Learn What The Bible Says About Marriage

Written and illustrated by Jeff Todd

A Marriage Built To Last:
Learn What The Bible Says About Marriage

Published by:
Jeff Todd
Newnan, Georgia

ISBN-13: 979-8-3304-9508-5

The purpose of this book is to share God's Word that relates to marriage and having healthy relationships. It is part of the outreach ministry of Jeff Todd.

Please note that there will be mistakes and misprints in this book. We are all human, right? We hope you won't find too many of them. This book was edited to the best of the author's ability and he will not be held responsible for errors.

Direct all correspondence to:

A BackPew Review
c/o Jeff Todd
PO Box 71972
Newnan, GA 30271-1972

Contents

Acknowledgements

This book is dedicated to my awesomely cool wife, Frances Todd, that won my heart back in the late 1980's with her beautiful eyes, wonderful smile and 4' 9" stature. Together, we've been through the good times and survived together through the bad times. I thank her for her strength, patience, love and being my life partner in this game called Life.

I also thank the Lord for joining us together on November 4th, 1989 and for keeping us together all of these years. We would not still be here today if it wasn't for Him.

For those of you thinking about marriage, I would take it seriously. Build your marriage foundation on God and allow Him to lead your new life together as a couple. He can make your marriage last and help you face the storms that life will bring.

And to those of you that are thinking about giving up on your marriage, I would give God a chance to fix what has been broken. If you and your spouse can join together in agreement to put God first in your life, He can mend you back together again.

My prayer is that this guide will help you in your quest for 'happily ever after'.

Reflection

I remember the first time I met her. I was sitting on the back pew of a small country church back home in Newnan, Georgia. I was just minding my own business and then, all of a sudden, she came along.

Just in case you're not familiar with the seating arrangements in a Southern church building, the back pew is a special place for church-goers. This was where all of the young 'hoodlums' of the church would sit and where most of the distracting noises during the services would come from. You knew it was the 'talking section' because the preacher would always look towards the back at you with a raised eyebrow. Sometimes he would preach louder when he felt that a part of his message was meant for you. This was usually followed by him pointing the Bible in your direction.

Anyway, I can't remember the exact day it was that we met, but I'm sure she does. And when she reads this, I can almost guarantee you that she will remind me of it. All I can remember is sitting on that back pew and seeing her eyes turn around to glance at me from four pews up for the very first time. It was a connection like I had never felt before. I had to meet her face to face.

To make a long story short, we ended up getting married about a year later in that same small church by that same preacher. It was the beginning of our life's journey together — just a couple of soul mates with a set of matching golden wedding rings. Happily ever after, right? Not hardly!

You see, you would think that the first year of marriage was easy. I mean, people in love can be broke as convicts and be living in a one-room shack and it not really matter. We're living on love! Right? It may have been like that for a little while, but something happens when you try to grow this relationship while adding the better paycheck, bigger home, a dependable car and a bunch of rugrats that look like the both of us. Stress enters in and the strength of this new relationship is tested. This is where some folks give up and they sign another contract together called a Divorce. Fortunately for us, we never took this direction.

The purpose of this book is to help couples out there by offering Biblical knowledge to marriage. The Bible is full of scripture that can help us in our relationships. However, many of us don't think to use it's wisdom as a guide. God put it there for us to use and wants us all to live happily ever after. We can also use those conflicts that enter our life in a positive way. Our marriages can be stronger by following God's plan. The Bible holds the answers.

Yes, my wife and I have been married since 1989, but it doesn't make either one of us an expert. We have been through good times and bad times, so the only thing we can offer is experience. I can also share with you what I have learned from the Bible and tell you that a marriage can only be as strong as it's foundation. In our case, we chose Jesus.

According to the grace of God which is given unto me, as a wise masterbuilder, I have laid the foundation, and another buildeth thereon. But let every man take heed how he buildeth thereupon. For other foundation can no man lay than that is laid, which is Jesus Christ. Now if any man build upon this foundation gold, silver, precious stones, wood, hay, stubble; every man's work shall be made manifest: for the day shall declare it, because it shall be revealed by fire; and the fire shall try every man's work of what sort it is. - 1 Corinthians 3: 10-13

Marriage takes work from both sides. It's just like building a house. You start out with a strong foundation and use quality materials. You're also going to roll your sleeves up and get your hands dirty. It takes patience and endurance because your love for each other will be tested with fire to see how it holds up. It's a lifelong process. That's just how it goes.

As a married couple in love, your relationship will go up against real life problems – financial, physical, mental and spiritual – to see if it's going to stand. This is how you tell if the 'love' is genuine because many couples today buckle under the pressure.

According to some statistics I found on the Internet, did you know that almost 50% of couples getting married in America will eventually end up in divorce? These are

mostly men and women aged 30 and younger. The sad thing is that the divorce rate is even higher for second and third marriages – roughly 60% ~ 70%. This is a serious issue!

We need to take a stand today and make every effort to stay together. The purpose of this book is to offer you help. My prayer is that it brings couples together and strengthens their relationship so that it will last forever – the way it was intended.

I hope it's a blessing to you.

Marriage

What Is Marriage?

What is marriage? That's a very good question and makes you do some thinking. Let me begin first by saying that it's not what Hollywood says it is or what the media tells us. Marriage isn't something you do and change your mind about whenever you feel like it, even though many people seem to think so. It isn't like a pair of underwear that you change once a week. If you can relate to that last

statement, you may have some major hygiene issues that needs to be corrected. You might want to get that checked out.

So, what is marriage anyway?

All that many of us know is that we teamed up with this person, fell In love, signed some paperwork and repeated a bunch of words in front of all these people. And then this fella says, "I pronounce you man and wife!"

The honeymoon was the best part, but it didn't last long. After that, it all seemed to go down hill from there. He changed. She changed. Now we're at each others throat and divorce seems to be the only solution. Whoever came up with the phrase 'happily ever after' must have been high because marriage doesn't have a fairy tale ending.

Wait!! Slow down and take a few breaths. Let's look back on the whole deal and recap what just happened. Let's go back to the starting point.

Before we can live happily ever after in our marriage with the one we love, we have to first know what we've gotten ourselves into. Let's do a quick walk-through of that special event.

We may remember signing a written contract and standing in front of a bunch of people all dressed up in suits and dresses. Right? We may remember repeating a long list of words given to us by a preacher as our knees shook and our hands got all sweaty and junk. Remember? Yeah, we put the golden ring on each others finger and said, "I do." But, it all happened so fast that maybe we didn't get the full scope on the target. Know what I mean? What did we just do?

Some folks will say we just signed our life away as if we just traded our 'freedom' for a life 'bound in chains' with a big iron ball attached to it. Others see it as new life being started; kinda like planting a seed in the ground and watching it bloom into several flowers that keeps on branching out and looking all pretty and all.

I've always liked that second description of marriage. But, I can also see why people see it more like the first one. When a couple gets married, they become one. So, they're kinda stuck together like a ball and chain, but it doesn't have to be like prison.

Our wedding day was awesome. My wife-to-be was so sweet and beautiful. Standing beside her in front of the preacher will be a day that I will never forget. And then, of course, the reception afterward when my new wife gave me my first commands of how I should and shouldn't act in public. The only person that ever told me 'what to do' was my mother. And now this new

person in my life is telling me what to do. I realized quickly that we had became one and that 'my' way of doing things affected her. I had to start early in making personal adjustments if I

wanted this thing to last. Plus, it was part of the deal we made on our wedding day.

One of the important things in marriage is those wedding vows. It's our promise and commitment we made to our spouse. Maybe we should begin first by looking at them. Do you remember everything you agreed to? Well, in case you forgot, here's a copy of those words you said on your wedding day. It may not be the exact words, but I'm sure it's pretty close. Let's check it out:

*I, **(your name here)**, take you **(your spouse's name here)**, to be my (wife/husband), to have and to hold from this day forward, for better or for worse, for richer, for poorer, in sickness and in health, to love and to cherish; from this day forward until death do us part.*

I know you were nervous and may not remember saying this stuff. If you were like me, your eyes may have been more focused on the person you were marrying and how great they looked. You may have wanted to get all this ceremonial stuff over with so that the two of you could proceed on to the honeymoon. Am I right?

But, believe it or not, those vows are very important. Keep in mind, you just repeated them in front of God and a bunch of people. These folks are witnesses to your words of commitment. You've signed the proper legal paperwork, exchanged the rings of unity and even dressed up for the occasion. You also sealed the deal with a kiss. You wouldn't do all of this special stuff for other contracts like buying a car or a house. Would you? I didn't think so. This is a special moment in time.

If a man vow a vow unto the Lord, or swear an oath to bind his soul with a bond; he shall not break his word, he shall do according to all that proceedeth out of his mouth. - Numbers 30: 2

By repeating those vows, you made a serious commitment. You undoubtedly loved this person so much that you were willing to get all dressed up and tell the world about it. You made a vow to this person in front of witnesses and was willing to slick your hair back and put on the 'smell-good stuff' to do it. This kind of thing doesn't happen every day.

And what about those vows? What's in them anyway? Let's go back to that special day and look at them a little more closely.

I know there are several variations to the wedding vow. For the most part, it all means the same thing. I chose to use the traditional version because this is the one that most people say. If your vow was different, you may want to go back and get a copy of it. Review it and make sure you understand what you agreed to.

Here's the traditional version:

I, (Your Name Here)

Just like in most agreements, you're stating your name first and letting folks in the audience know who you are. You are putting your name on the line. This includes your reputation as someone that sticks to a contract. If you're a person that breaks agreements easily, the witnesses in the audience already realize this and are probably only attending your wedding for the refreshments and party afterward. They know they will get invited to the next one.

A good name is rather to be chosen than great riches, and loving favour rather than silver and gold. - Proverbs 22: 1

But, if you're a person of your word, then this agreement is serious business. You know that your reputation is at risk if you break the deal.

Take You (Your Spouse's Name Here)

This is the person you are committing to. By marrying this person, you are simply saying that, out of all the people in the world, you chose them to become 'one' with and that your love for them is the real deal.

For me, there's not too many people I would be willing to put a suit on for. My wife just so happens to be one of them. Our wedding day was special to me, so I went all out for the occasion. I

rented the best tux I could find – which was only from one store in Smalltown, GA – but I added some extra bling like the duck tail sport coat and even bought socks that matched. I knew that the girl I was marrying would be the only one. There wouldn't be any other after this.

To Be My (Wife/Husband)

Being a wife or a husband is more than a title. Yeah, I know it sounds kinda good and all, but it's more than that. It's a responsibility and a commitment that says that 'you're the only one for me'. When you take someone to be your spouse, you're basically letting them into your spiritual

circle so that the two of you can be molded into one. Does that make sense?

Therefore shall a man leave his father and his mother, and shall cleave unto his wife: and they shall be one flesh. - Genesis 2: 24

It's great that either the wife or husband that you chose just so happens to be a great cook or does a great job at working on the car. But, that's just an added bonus. That's physical stuff. I'm talking about spiritual oneness! That's what marriage is really about.

To Have and To Hold From This Day Forward

To have and to hold? I like the 'holding' part, but 'to have' sounds more like ownership with a paper receipt that you can frame on your wall. I don't like the way that rolls off my fingertips onto this computer screen. What's that all about?

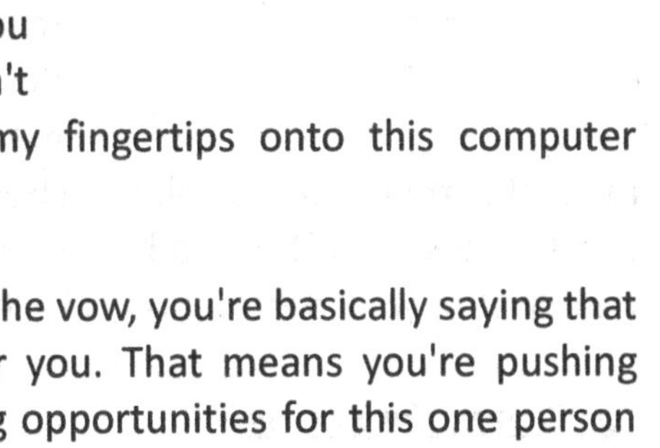

When you repeat this part of the vow, you're basically saying that they will be the only one for you. That means you're pushing aside all of those other dating opportunities for this one person that you are making a commitment to. And this promise begins the day you say, "I do."

Some married couples take the 'to have' to the extreme. They feel that they own their spouse. This isn't the way it should be. Marriage is about being together and working together as a team like a partnership. That marriage certificate isn't a deed to a tract of land. This is a relationship that involves two people that truly love each other – and no one else.

For Better or For Worse

Marriage is intended to be a permanent thing and shouldn't fluctuate with the changing scenery. In good times and bad times, your marriage commitment should stick like Super Glue.

What if a tire decided to pop off your truck because it was hot outside? I mean, one of the tires got a little hot under the pressure and says, "Pheww! I need to sit this one out. Ya'll handle this on your own!" It wouldn't work.

It takes the work of all of the tires to make it move forward to it's destination. The same is true in marriage, it takes both of you to make this thing successful. You should work together through the good times and the bad. You have to pull your own load. Remember, your destination is to 'forever'. Right?

For Richer, For Poorer

Money shouldn't be an issue in the marriage, but it is. Money seems to be one of the major reasons people get divorced. But, according to the wedding vows, a couple agrees that no matter how rich or poor they are, they will stick together and tough it out.

A great way to test the 'money theory' is to imagine your spouse without an income. Could you still love them? Would you be willing to support them with the money you earn? According to the vow, you said you would.

Or how do you feel about combining both incomes into a joint bank account? Do you feel that what's 'his is his' or 'hers is hers'? For a marriage to flow in a positive direction, you should put it together and discuss your finances together as a team.

Men and women see money in different ways. I guess that's why they say opposites attract. Men tend to see money as a scorecard and treat it as a goal to accumulate as much of it as they can. That's why many of them lose self-esteem when there's money issues in the home. They may feel responsible for not being able to provide more for the family. Women, on the other hand, tend to see money as a source of security. When money issues occur, many of them react in fear. They may lash out at their husbands for being in such a financial mess. This in turn may make him lash out because of his feeling of helplessness.

You have to go back to the wedding vows and remember that you both promised to stick together no matter what your balance is in your bank account. Take the focus off of the funds and put them on God and each other.

For the love of money is the root of all evil: which while some coveted after, they have erred from the faith, and pierced themselves through with many sorrows. - 1 Timothy 6: 10

But my God shall supply all your need according to his riches in glory by Christ Jesus. - Philippians 4: 19

Money was a struggle for me in our first year of marriage because I was young, selfish and the main financial provider at the time. I felt that I 'earned' it and that it belonged to me. I couldn't understand why I had to spend money that I worked hard for on disposable feminine products that my wife needed. This didn't make sense to me. In my mind, this was money wasted that could have been used on better stuff like dice that hangs on your truck mirror or a set of wrenches. Those things made sense, but not girl stuff. No way!

I know that sounds funny now, but at the time, that was a real-life crisis for me. I'm glad I matured and realized that everything from that day forward is 'ours' and not 'mine'. I also learned that God is our Provider and that we are to be stewards of what He has given us, regardless of who in the marriage He chooses to give it to.

In Sickness and in Health

When a married couple is healthy and living life normally, there may not be any problems in the marriage in this area. But, what if one of them becomes sick? What if it got to the point to where they were bed ridden and the other spouse had to take the full load of the home?

Could you stay married to that person you love if they were stricken down with a terrible disease? According to the vow we made, we told them we would always be there no matter what.

I remember our first year of marriage. One day, my brand new wife caught a virus and became sick. One morning she decided to puke right there on the floor of our 4-room shack because she couldn't make it to the bathroom. It was messy and gross. For a minute, I looked at her and hoped she would get that up, but I quickly saw that she wasn't able. I had a decision to make. I could either let that stuff dry up and let her scrape it up when she got to feeling better or I could just love her like I said I did and take care of her while she was sick. Let's just say I held my breath and proceeded with the clean-up.

I learned that taking care of my wife was part of the marriage contract we made together. This involved a sacrifice on my part.

So ought men to love their wives as their own bodies. He that loveth his wife loveth himself. - Ephesians 5: 28

Marriage is about sacrificing and taking the load of our spouse when they aren't able. If we truly love them, we can do it.

To Love and To Cherish
Love and cherish are words that almost mean the same thing.

Love - To have a deep, tender, indescribable feeling of affection and concern toward someone.

Cherish - To treat with affection and tenderness; hold dear.

Love has so many levels and cherish, being one of it's forms, would mean to have affection for that person to the point that you want them protected. Basically, you have placed a high value on them in your life. This is how we should treat our spouses.

Would you toss a valuable painting by Van Gogh around like a Frisbee? Would you take an expensive sports car through a mud hole? Of course not. Unless you live in my neck of the woods because anything you take through the mud means you actually cherish it. But, hopefully, you get the idea.

We should treat our spouses like we would a priceless treasure. I have been guilty of not cherishing my wife as I should. Here's an example:

I am a little bit scared of bats. OK, I'll tell the truth. Bats totally freak me out! They're squirmy rats with wings and they make my skin crawl.

My wife and I decided to save some money on our electric bill during the Summer and chose to sleep with our windows open instead of running our air conditioner. It worked, but it came with a price. You know all those creepy things that live outside? Well, with windows open, they now have a way of getting inside.

One night, a bat decided to let itself in. He was fluttering around in our bedroom, banging against the walls and it woke us up. My wife cuts the light on and we see him. He's scary looking! I freak out and I'm screaming! I jump out of bed and run for shelter. Without thinking, I grab my wife and hide behind her. I use her like a shield from this terrible beast that's about to turn me into a vampire. The battle wages as we use every household item to drive this beast out of our home. After a few terrifying hours, he finally leaves. We are finally safe! All we are left with is a recap of the night's events. I realized I broke a wedding vow. I put my wife in harms way in order to protect myself. That's selfish.

Because if I truly cherished her, I probably would've tried to protect her instead of using her. I wouldn't have used her as a shield in the face of danger. However, in a bat situation, I can't promise that I won't do this again. But, I will work on it.

The Bible tells us:

<u>For the men:</u>
Husbands, love your wives, even as Christ also loved the church, and gave himself for it. - Ephesians 5: 25

How much does Jesus love the church? He gave His life for it. That's pretty deep right there. How far are you willing to go for your wife?

Taking out the garbage every day or turning off that football game to spend time with your wife is a minor thing. Listening to her thoughts and providing some feedback is a minor thing, too. Actually, sacrificing yourself and time to make sure her emotional and physical needs are taken care of doesn't come close to what Jesus did for us. Giving of ourselves to our wives is the least we could do.

Nevertheless let every one of you in particular so love his wife even as himself; and the wife see that she reverence her husband. - Ephesians 5: 33

To have reverence means to have respect. Women should respect their husbands by being in tune with their emotions and needs. Be concerned and do what it takes to build them up. They should also let them know how much they are appreciated and be sincere about it. Ladies, we can tell the difference.

If we have accomplished something that we're proud enough to tell you about, get excited, too. Mark it down on the calendar and create a family holiday around it and celebrate it every year. Bake a cake and decorate it with sugar sprinkles. Buy some balloons to let us know you care. That's all we need.

From This Day Forward Until Death Do Us Part

Marriage has an expiration date – it's death. As sad as it may sound, there will come a day when either you or your spouse will die. It's just how life goes and we don't know which one will be first to go. When it does happen, the marriage vow you made will have been fulfilled. This tells me that we should work hard together to make marriage something that will bring us happiness and peace because we are in it until the end. Every obstacle we face in marriage should be something we should try to fix together instead of using it as an excuse to separate.

But when death does come, it doesn't mean that both of you have to die. The spouse that's living should continue living and they can even though the other has passed away. It then becomes a choice of whether they want to enter in another contract with someone else.

Personally, you may have had such a bad experience with the last deal that you may not want to do it again. Or you have a hard time dealing with being lonely that you need someone else in your life. It's OK. Go for it!

And the Lord God said, It is not good that the man should be alone; I will make him an help meet for him. - Genesis 2:18

Marriage is about a partnership — two bodies becoming one. The key to having a marriage that lasts forever is to let death be the only thing that separates you. If it happens, it's OK to move on. God doesn't want us to live life alone and will put someone else in your life if you want Him to.

Love

Puppy Love

Do you remember many years ago as a young child falling in love with someone? I know. It's been awhile. But if you remember, falling in love back then was usually started by one of your friends telling you that this person thinks you're cute. The next thing you know is that there's a love letter involved that asks the question, "Do you love me? Check YES or NO." Remember those? I'm sure you've written a few of them. The real good ones were the ones that were folded all cool and junk with the little flappy thing for easy opening. It may have had some perfume or cologne squirted on it for extra flair.

Checking YES didn't really take that much effort and was really determined by how cute you thought they were. You definitely wasn't concerned about their financial status, criminal background or mental stability. Those things didn't really even matter back then. It was all about how cute they were and how good you would look in front of your friends by hanging out with them. Am I right?

This person became your boyfriend or girlfriend automatically when you checked YES on their introduction letter. This was followed up with an awkward personal confrontation where neither one of you knew what to say. And then there's that series of daily love letters that you passed back and forth every day. In addition, there were those phone calls that lasted for hours that totally drove your parents insane. If you had cool parents, they would take the both of you out

on a date and cover the costs. Most of the time dating was done only at school in the hallway.

Over time, the newness wore off and another person came along and said the right things that made us all gooey inside. We would break up with our current boyfriend or girlfriend and start the whole process all over again. It was as if the other boyfriend or girlfriend never really even mattered. They were made history so quickly because it was time for us to move on. But, didn't we say we loved them? What happened? The sad thing is that some marriages are being treated like this today.

Teenage 'puppy' love is almost like true love except that it can change in a sudden moment. Just because I love you today, you might say something I don't like or act in way that ticks me off and immediately I won't love you anymore. That's puppy love.

Puppy love is common among teenagers. Parents realize what puppy love is and how quickly this love can change between a couple. Parents get accused of being too strict or called dictators for wanting to get involved in their kid's love life. Even though teens feel that their love is real, parents know the truth about love and have experienced it. That's why they do everything in their power to protect their kids when it comes to dating. They have to be cautious when they allow them to leave their home because teens are made mostly of raging sexual hormones. They could end up doing something stupid and pay a price for it for the rest of their life.

Teenagers in 'love' with a driver's license need supervision. This 'freedom' may mean they are able to date more and do more exciting things. However, because they are away from their parent's view, they are liable to do almost anything. Parents try to protect them, while at the same time, allow them space and freedom to date. Trust

becomes the issue between a parent and their teen. That's why teens should follow their parent's strict guidelines:

"Call me and let me know where you're at every hour on the hour. Got it?"

"I want you home by 10:00 pm, no excuses!"

"When I was a kid, the boy always paid for the date. This is how you separate the real boys from the losers."

"Before I let you date him, I want to meet him in person – face to face."

"I'm going with you! I'll sit in the backseat."

And the list goes on and on. Teenagers may not understand why their parents give them these rules to follow. They may see it as dumb. The fact is, parents are protecting their child's future. Puppy love is dangerous because it can make a couple do things that they would later regret. Parents with dating rules for their teens actually care.

Dating is fun and very important. A young couple can learn more about each other. This will either draw them closer together in their relationship or push them away. This is a very important stage for teenage boys and girls. It's best to know each other first. You don't want to spend a lifetime with someone you really don't know. Do you?

This leads to another topic in their relationship — SEX. Sex is a common thing for teenagers to do in society during the dating game. It's almost a guarantee for any teenage couple left unattended for any length of time. I feel it's not a good idea to do it because what if they get pregnant by someone they haven't even learned about yet? They don't know if this person is the one they want to spend the rest of their life with. Now they have a baby stuck in the middle. What do they do now?

This is where the word ABSTINENCE comes into play; choosing not to have sex before marriage. I know - it's not popular.

Abstinence involves strength and courage from both parties, especially knowing how much peer pressure there will be into giving in. The reward for staying pure will be well worth it in the end. This usually happens after you're married. There's just something peaceful about knowing you're the only person your spouse has ever had. This prevents any future jealousy that occurs in many marriages today. The worse thing that could happen in a marriage relationship is for your spouse to hold up a scorecard after having sex. This would mean they judged your performance based on their past experiences. Competition isn't a good

thing in a situation like this. It leads to arguments.

Nevertheless, to avoid fornication, let every man have his own wife, and let every woman have her own husband. - 1 Corinthians 7: 2

Fornication is one of them big words mentioned in the Bible and it simply means consensual sexual intercourse between two persons not married to each other.

Here's what can happen to teenagers that choose to have sex before marriage:

1. They can catch a sexually transmitted disease. It's possible. There's a lot of cooties floating around out there. You don't want to catch one of them because some of that stuff is hard to wash off. Some diseases can even kill you.
2. They could learn to love each other, get married and live happily ever after. It happens and it could be that they were meant to be together. Sex before marriage may not have an impact on them at all.
3. They could become pregnant. Any time you play with fire, there's a chance of getting burned. What are the choices of a teenage couple faced with a baby on the way? Here's a few:
- They could go ahead and have the baby and learn that they're not compatible. They would separate and the baby would be born not having a healthy relationship with it's mother or father.
- They could have the baby and learn to love each other, get married and live happily ever after. Of course, they would have to explain later to their child why Mama's belly seemed to take up most of the picture in their

wedding photos. I'm sure they'll come up with something.

- Choosing not to keep it comes with two options: having an abortion or giving it up for adoption. This choice will make a huge impact on the lives of everyone involved. Some people have years later regretted making either one of them.

There are too many risks when it comes to having sex in a relationship. The main concern is the child that could be born in the process. We have to add him or her to the equation. And importantly, we need to make sure the person we're having sex with is someone we want to spend a lifetime with for the child's sake. There are too many kids out there that will never know who their parents are and will suffer the scars for the rest of their life.

It's best to know the difference between puppy love and true love. Taking our parent's advice would be a great idea.

True Love

True love is something you only hear about in fairy tales, right? Nope. It actually exists.

However, I don't believe you find it in the beginning. You may love this person or have feelings for them, but to truly love them is more than just a feeling. It's an action that is seen in how we act towards them. Don't get discouraged. Over time, this love can grow to become true love, but it requires the effort of both people in the relationship.

It's like growing a garden that begins with a small seed and two gardeners. If it's a seed that both feel are worth planting, they will each take a part in helping it spring to life and produce fruit. This would be similar to tilling the ground, planting the seed, fertilizing the soil, giving it sunlight and watering it. Occasionally weeds will come in and try to kill the plant. The couple will need to work together to get rid of them.

The perfect place to learn about true love is from the Bible (*1 Corinthians 13: 4-8a):*

- Love is patient
- Love is kind
- Love doesn't envy

- Love doesn't boast
- Love isn't proud
- Love isn't rude
- Love isn't self-seeking
- Love isn't easily angered
- Love doesn't keep records of wrong
- Love doesn't delight in evil
- Love rejoices with the truth
- Love always protects
- Love always trusts
- Love always hopes
- Love always perseveres
- Love never fails

That's why the 'dating period' is so important. It allows a couple time to learn more about each other to see if they are compatible. Remember, your goal is to spend the rest of your life with them. Choose wisely.

For the record, here's what true love IS NOT. It shouldn't include any of the following:

- violence
- deception
- abuse (emotional, physical or verbal)
- constant sacrifice for the good of only one person
- jealousy
- fear
- mistrust

Sayin',
"I Do."

So, You Think You're Ready For Marriage, Huh?

I imagine you've been dating this person enough and feel they could be the one for you. Right?

Are you willing to push aside everyone else for this one person that you want to spend the rest of your life with? How about getting rid of that Black Book that contains all of those phone numbers of potential candidates for dating? Yeah? Wow! You must really be serious about taking the big step. Awesome!

Before you jump into this lifelong marriage thing, let's answer a few questions. It would be great if the both of you could answer YES to these:

1. Do you care about each other?

2. Do you have respect for each others needs?

    Nevertheless let every one of you in particular so love his wife even as himself; and the wife see that she reverence her husband – Ephesians 5: 33

3. Do you have great communication going on between each other?

4. Are you honest with each other on big and small issues?

    The integrity of the upright shall guide them: but the perverseness of transgressors shall destroy them. - Proverbs 11: 3

5. Are you committed to each other and this relationship you have?

    Be strong and of a good courage, fear not, nor be afraid of them: for the LORD thy God, he it is that doth go with thee; he will not fail thee, nor forsake thee. - Deuteronomy 31: 6

How did you do on the answers? Could the both of you agree on all of them? If so, that's awesome! Just know that from the day you say I DO, your marriage will be tested with fire to see how it holds up. It's these tests that will either break or make your relationship stronger. It would be a great idea to make sure you are building it on a strong foundation.

By following Jesus as a couple, you are given strength to weather the storms that are guaranteed to come into your life. The lessons and values from His Word are there to help you as long as you actually apply them.

A Quick Test

Here are some tidbits to look out for before making that big plunge into the deep waters of marriage. These are things that could jeopardize the marriage. Do either of you:

1) drink too much?
2) spend too much?
3) work too much?
4) brag too much?
5) use drugs?
6) get involved in illegal stuff?

These things become major topics in arguments between married couples and should be removed. It would be great to get this stuff settled and out of the way before entering a lifelong agreement with each other.

Finding Mr/Mrs Right

Did you find Mr/Mrs Right? Well, let's examine some of their traits:

1. Do they make you feel good about yourself?
2. Do you feel safe around them?
3. Is your life fulfilled because of them?
4. Are they positive thinkers and doers?
5. Do they put your emotions and physical needs first?

6. Do they encourage you and make you feel good about yourself?
7. Do they express their love for you, not only in words, but in actions?
8. Do you consider them also as a friend?
9. Are they kind, considerate and polite towards you?
10. Do they want the same things out of life as you do?
11. Are they open to share their feelings and thoughts with you?

If you answered YES to all of these, it sounds like you have found the right one for you. This is someone that you can work with and grow a marriage together with that can last a long time. Go for it! Together, you will face storms in life that will rattle the chains of your relationship. The key is to stay true to each other, love each other and face problems together as they come. As long as you keep your partner's best interests in mind first (before your own), everything is going to work out fine.

Let nothing be done through strife or vainglory; but in lowliness of mind let each esteem other better than themselves. Look not every man on his own things, but every man also on the things of others. - Philippians 2: 3, 4

Our Roles In The Marriage
Each of us has a responsibility in our marriage. It shouldn't be one-sided. It takes two to make things work. No one should be

trying to handle it all on their own.

Some people think that marriage consists of:

The man's role (Old Way Of Thinking):
The man works, comes home, eats and watches TV. He repeats this daily and the weekends belong to him to do as he pleases.

Additional duties: He maintains the yard, vehicles and disciplines the children after the woman has screamed, yelled and pulled most of her hair out. His income goes into the bank and is spent by the woman. However, she must save some as a weekly allowance for the man to spend on his leisure activities such as hunting, fishing and working on his hobby cars parked in the yard (which could remain parked there for the full length of the marriage).

The woman's role (Old Way Of Thinking):
The woman stays home, cleans the house, raises the kids, cooks and spends the household money. She also caters to the man's emotional and physical needs upon request. His needs will require immediate attention on her part.

Additional duties: She maintains the law and order in the home by nagging, whining and complaining. She also buys the groceries, household items and personal stuff she needs. She can spend as many hours (or days) as needed to achieve her weekly goal at the local Wally World. Buying more than one of something is acceptable as long as it's on sale or if she has a coupon for it.

All of this may be cool in the beginning of the marriage, but over time folks are going to get burned out and be completely miserable. It may seem like the workload in the home isn't evenly distributed and I'm sure it's not.

As we already know, the basics for a healthy lifestyle in a home can be summarized in 5 categories:

- **Maintain an income**
- **Pay bills**
- **Maintain the home**
- **Strengthen the marriage relationship**
- **Develop the children into upstanding citizens through discipline and love**

This is pretty much what has to be done on a daily basis. So who gets what job? What does the Bible say about how a home should be ran? What are our roles in the marriage?

<u>For the man (Biblical View):</u>

1. He is to be the leader

For the husband is the head of the wife, even as Christ is the head of the church: and he is the saviour of the body. - Ephesians 5: 23

The men are to be leaders in the home. This does not mean that he is to be a dictator. This doesn't give them the right to boss people around. Actually, he should live a life that makes people want to follow him. He has to be the example to his wife and children with a lifestyle that reflects Jesus.

He should be willing to help his wife as a partner in all that they do. If Jesus was willing to wash His disciple's feet, then we (as men) should be willing to help wash the dishes after dinner. Especially if our wives work at a job during the day just like we do. Know what I mean? Being a leader means 'making the steps first' in all areas of the home and the relationship.

2. He is to love his wife

Husbands, love your wives, even as Christ also loved the church, and gave himself for it – Ephesians 5: 25

Husbands, love your wives, and be not bitter against them. - Colossians 3: 19

Because of this love a man should have for his wife, his leadership should reflect it. This means he wouldn't make sudden decisions without talking it over with her. He will think as a team and not all about himself. Based on scripture, we are to give of ourselves to our wives just as Jesus did for the church.

For the woman (Biblical View):

1. She should submit to her husband

Therefore as the church is subject unto Christ, so let the wives be to their own husbands in every thing. - Ephesians 5: 24

Wives, submit yourselves unto your own husbands, as it is fit in the Lord. - Colossians 3: 18

Being submissive doesn't make the woman weak or unable to speak her opinions because the scripture relating to the husband is about how he should 'love' her. Good stuff is working both ways for the husband and the wife. To 'submit' means to voluntarily put yourself in the hands of another. I'm sure this is very hard to do, but it's scriptural and wouldn't be in there if it didn't help the marriage. I believe as long as there's no abuse, violence behavior and the man is going the direction that Lord is taking him, then the woman shouldn't have a problem with it. Actually, it could take some of the stress off of her. She could then pray for him and ask the Lord to direct his paths because his direction as a leader involves her, too. Plus, if a bad decision is made, she could blame it on her husband. I'm just joking on that last part.

2.   She should help her husband

And the LORD God said, It is not good that the man should be alone; I will make him an help meet for him. - Genesis 2: 18

This is what being a wife boils down to right here. She is a helpmate to the husband. They're a team of two working together towards the same life goals. This is how you achieve 'happily ever after' in the marriage. The key word in this is 'help' and men need all the help they can get.

Maybe in the old days, it was great that the man went to work and provided the income to pay the bills. In those days, men were paid more than women, so it was practical for him to work. And because of the economy and the family's frugal spending, his income may have been sufficient to cover all of the expenses. This would allow the woman to stay home and take care of the house and the children. Believe it or not, a homemaker is a real job. It just doesn't get the recognition it deserves.

But by doing it this way, it was considered a 50/50 split and the rest of their time could be spent strengthening their marriage and spending quality time with their kids.

In today's society, one income isn't enough unless you're a doctor, lawyer or rocket scientist. In most cases, it takes two. So, how do you manage everything? Well, you have to apply time management principles. Time should be split 50/50 and you work together doing the things on the Daily To Do List. Each person has

strengths and weaknesses when it comes to managing the family. The stronger one should handle the jobs that are best suited for them. Everyone should be busy doing something. We should stay away from the belief that 'it's a man's job' or 'it's a woman's job' to do certain things. Instead, we should say, "It's OUR job as a married couple working together. We're a team."

In my earlier years of marriage, we had the 'old school' mentality. I worked and my wife stayed home and did all of the things that sweet little wives did. She cooked. She cleaned. But, she never took out the trash. She would always say, "That's a man's job!" and allow it to overflow into the floor. I could never really grasp the concept behind that way of thinking. It's household garbage. It's part of the house. If she maintains the house, then why couldn't she be the one to take it out? What are we talking about here? 5 minutes of physical labor? It didn't make sense to me.

Now we know that marriage is about working together and simply doing what we can in our strengths to accomplish our daily goals. It's teamwork!

Knowing all of this should help your marriage last longer and survive the hard times. Saying I DO at the end of your wedding vows means being the one to step up to the plate in saying I WILL when it comes to things related to your marriage.

Sayin', "I Quit."

Fixin' The Problems In Marriage

If you're reading this part of the book, you may be in a marriage that has now lost it's fire. You've been thinking about divorce as an option and maybe starting all over again. However, there's a part of you that's thinking there may be some hope. If you didn't, you wouldn't be reading this book at all.

So, before we go to the extreme and get a lawyer and sign a bunch of paperwork, let's see if there's something that can rekindle that flame you once had in the very beginning. All it takes is a spark to start a fire, right?

Maybe we can take a look at the problems that occur in a marriage and see if the Bible has solutions for it. To me, that would be the best place to start.

What therefore God hath joined together, let not man put asunder.
- Mark 10: 9

Since God invented the whole marriage thing, I would almost guarantee that He has something in there that could keep the marriage together as long as we applied what it said. But, first and foremost, we need to make sure we are truly living for Him. We should pray and ask for forgiveness of any junk that may hinder our relationship with Him.

Secondly, for His solutions to work, both people in the relationship must work at this together. It's a team effort.

Ask yourselves:

- Do we love each other?
- Do we want this marriage to work?
- Are we willing to do whatever it takes to get back on track?
- Regardless of who we think is in the wrong, are we willing to forgive each other?

If the both of you could answer YES to these questions, you have what it takes to save your marriage. That is awesome!

Now let's see what the Bible says.

Money

Money issues ranks as one of the top reasons couples argue in the marriage. In many cases, this leads to divorce. According to statistics, 50% of marriages will eventually end up this way and money problems seem to be the main cause. What is it about money that destroys relationships? It could be how we prioritize it in our life. How does it rank on your ladder of important stuff?

Healthy Priorities

1. **God**

   God should rank number one in our life and relationship. If you're married and teeter-tottering on the edge of divorce, now would be a great time to move Him to the top of your list. You need Him because He is your Provider, Helper and the One that's going to keep your marriage together.

2. **Our Spouse**

   This is your partner and soul mate. This is the person you made the vow to in the beginning and promised to love no matter what changes take place in your environment. This relationship should be unconditional.

3. **Our Kids**

   These are the cute by-products of the love you have with your spouse. Believe it or not, they are temporary fixtures in your home that will one day move on and start families of their own. Some take longer to move on than others. Your goal is to guide and direct them and get them off your couch.

4. **Money and Other Stuff**

   Everything else in life is at the bottom of the priority list.

You can probably arrange things in this category however you want. These things aren't as important as the first three.

Prioritizing is important in having a healthy marriage. If you make any sudden adjustments, it can blow things out of proportion. This will create arguments and things can get out of control to the point of divorce. We don't want that to happen, do we?

I know in my many years of marriage, I've let priorities get out of whack. I would put money at the top and my wife at the bottom. Or I would put God at the bottom and my job at the top. You can always tell when priorities aren't where they should be – this is when arguments happen or when your prayers and spiritual life suffers.

Now that money has caused a stink in the marriage, it's time to look for solutions from the Bible to get things squared up. There are three arguments about money. We'll try and take one at a time.

Debt

Debt is created when we borrow money from someone or something like a financial institution such as a bank. They make it easy for us by

providing us with those cool plastic cards for swiping. If you look around in the world today, it seems like everybody has one. They look like a bunch of Credit Card Ninjas out there swiping junk. The problem is that we are spending money that we don't own –

it's other people's money. We're basically saying that we will pay them back and give them a little extra for letting us use it. They're hoping we won't be able to so that they can charge us more in penalties and whatever else they can put at the end of our credit card statements every month.

This creates a problem in the marriage because one or both parties are borrowing more than what the couple earns in wages. They're broke because they're overspent. Now they are working harder to pay back loans. This is stressful and it shouldn't be this way. God's plan is simple:

Owe no man any thing, but to love one another: for he that loveth another hath fulfilled the law. - Romans 13: 8

The only debt we should owe is the debt of love. We shouldn't borrow, except for the purchase of a house (which according to the Old Testament, the loan should have been a 7 year note without interest – read Deuteronomy 15).

The key is to be content with what you have.

For we brought nothing into this world, and it is certain we can carry nothing out. And having food and raiment let us be therewith content. But they that will be rich fall into temptation and a snare, and into many foolish and hurtful lusts, which drown men in destruction and perdition. For the love of money is the root of all evil: which while some coveted after, they have erred from the faith, and pierced themselves through with many sorrows. - 1 Timothy 6: 7-10

Spending
Spending is similar to the debt topic above with one exception – you're not borrowing money to buy stuff. You are actually using money you've earned to make purchases. The problem is that you may be using money that should have been used for other things such as paying bills. This creates problems in the marriage because it weakens the financial security in the home. Everybody is on edge because the bills are coming in and there's no funds to pay for them. There should be because together you made enough to cover them, but somebody used those funds on something else. The root of the problem is the need to accumulate stuff. Here again the solution is contentment.

But godliness with contentment is great gain. - 1 Timothy 6: 6

If we focus more on living a life that is pleasing to God, we learn to be content with what we have. It doesn't mean we are settling for second-best or having to live a life in poverty. It means that we will start looking at the things we already own in a new perspective. Our values will change. The way we

handle money will change. We become good stewards with what the Lord has given us, and according to the scripture, this is great gain.

Combining The Money

One of the problems with money in the marriage is the willingness to combine incomes. Some couples don't want to add their money together into a joint bank account. They would rather work as a separate entity when it comes to the financial stuff. Why is that?

Is it a trust issue? Do they feel that the other person will be foolish with it and blow it on something stupid? It could be. However, it's hard to have a healthy marriage with trust issues percolating in money pot.

What's the solution?

It's knowing that God is in control and is the Provider. Yes, we may work and earn the paycheck, but it is ultimately God who opened the door. Know what I'm saying? All of it belongs to Him. He's in charge.

But my God shall supply all your need according to his riches in glory by Christ Jesus. - Philippians 4: 19

If both people are working as a team in the marriage, then the trust issue should be discussed. Iron it out, pray about it and allow God to work with them to fix it. This will require faith.

Let your conversation be without covetousness; and be content with such things as ye have: for he hath said, I will never leave thee, nor forsake thee. - Hebrews 13: 5

Adultery

Thou shalt not commit adultery. - Exodus 20: 14

God must have been serious about a man and woman staying together forever because He included the command *'thou shalt not commit adultery'* to the Ten Commandments. He may have known that healthy relationships work better when only two people are involved. It gets a bit confusing when you add a third, fourth or fifth party to the love equation. Maybe that's why adultery is one of the reasons for divorce today.

What exactly is adultery? And why is it such a bad thing anyway? Dictionaries tell us that it's voluntary sexual intercourse between a married person and someone other than the lawful spouse. Lawful spouse? Say what?

According to the law, you entered a legal agreement. A person that commits adultery is breaking the law. Breaking the law makes them a criminal that could serve jail time for their actions. That's some serious stuff!

If that wasn't enough to wake a person up, there's also a spiritual issue when it comes to adultery.

But whoso committeth adultery with a woman lacketh understanding: he that doeth it destroyeth his own soul. - Proverbs 6: 32

Adultery destroys an innocent spouse, innocent children, family relationships, it can spread disease, it can result in kids being born out-of-wedlock and can ruin a person's reputation in a community. It's a destructive path that many choose to take.

According to the Bible, not only is it a sexual thing, we can also commit adultery by lusting with our eyes and heart.

Based on that, we have to be careful what we allow our eyes to see. Things such as X-rated movies and porn magazines aren't harmless. These things would add fuel to the fire. It's best to get rid of it for the sake of the marriage.

Marriage is honourable in all, and the bed undefiled: but whoremongers and adulterers God will judge. - Hebrews 13: 4

It's a serious thing regardless of what society thinks by making it look like the latest fad. It goes against God. And you don't want to do that!

What would make a married person want to cheat on their spouse when they have everything they need right there in their home? Here are the five most popular reasons:

- They feel neglected
- They have low self-esteem
- They seek excitement
- Their spouse works too much – no time for play
- They fell out of love

I was going to write a few paragraphs about each reason, but realized that they are all pretty much related. The solution is to go back to our list of priorities in life.

1. **God**
2. **Our Spouse**
3. **Our Kids**
4. **Money and Other Stuff**

Our spouse should be our top priority in life under God. They should be what we think about first thing in the morning. We should focus on the things that we could do to make them happy. It's natural for people to be self-centered and to want the things that will satisfy us, but marriage is a spiritual thing. We would have to respond in the opposite way we would naturally think by giving of ourselves, especially to our spouses. Here are a few examples:

- *Spend more time with the one you love.*
- *Get involved with the things they like to do.*
- *Let them know they're important to you.*
- *Build your partner up – be an encourager.*
- *Love - show and tell them.*
- *Make the marriage fun.*
- *Go out on dates.*
- *Do something adventurous together.*
- *Take more vacations with your spouse.*

- *Practice working less. Free up time so that it can be spent with your spouse.*
- *Cut back on your expenses so that you don't have to work so much.*
- *Rekindle those flames of love.*
- *Go back to the time when you both first met and reenact some of those lost moments in time.*

Create your own list of things you could do. Get creative!

For the married couple where one of them has cheated on their spouse, staying married is a choice that both of them will have to agree on. The Bible mentions that adultery (fornication) is a legitimate reason for divorce.

But I say unto you, That whosoever shall put away his wife, saving for the cause of fornication, causeth her to commit adultery: and whosoever shall marry her that is divorced committeth adultery. - Matthew 5: 32

Whosoever putteth away his wife, and marrieth another, committeth adultery: and whosoever marrieth her that is put away from her husband committeth adultery. - Luke 16: 18

However, married couples can work through this problem in their marriage. It takes time to rebuild that trust. If both love each other and are willing to work together, then they should. This may involve starting over like newlyweds and removing any obstacles that stand in their way.

Abuse

No one should feel like they have to stay in an abusive marriage – whether it's verbal, emotional or physical. It doesn't matter! It's unhealthy. The Bible tells us:

Marriage is honourable in all
– Hebrews 13: 4a

This means marriage is something we should honor. Married couples should love and respect each other. Period.

If a person truly loved their spouse, they would want what's best for them. For the Christian marriage where abuse is present, it could be that the abuser doesn't know God. Maybe they're unsaved.

He that loveth not knoweth not God; for God is love. - 1 John 4: 8

Here are the characteristics of someone that knows how to love their spouse from 1 Corinthians 13: 4-8a:

- Love is patient
- Love is kind
- Love doesn't envy
- Love doesn't boast
- Love isn't proud
- Love isn't rude
- Love isn't self-seeking
- Love isn't easily angered
- Love doesn't keep records of wrong
- Love doesn't delight in evil
- Love rejoices with the truth
- Love always protects
- Love always trusts
- Love always hopes
- Love always perseveres
- Love never fails

For Christian married couples out there that aren't receiving this type of love from their spouse, I would question their partner's salvation. It's not of God. Something just ain't right.

The problem that occurs in relationships like this is that the abused spouse still loves the abuser. If it's a so-called Christian relationship, the abused feels obligated to stay married because scripture seems to frown against divorce with exceptions to adultery. They may feel trapped to stay in the marriage and take the abuse.

It hath been said, Whosoever shall put away his wife, let him give her a writing of divorcement: but I say unto you, That whosoever shall put away his wife, saving for the cause of fornication, causeth her to commit adultery: and whosoever shall marry her that is divorced committeth adultery. - Matthew 5: 31, 32

First of all, this isn't the marriage that God originally created. He wanted marriages to last a lifetime. But, because of man's hardened hearts, He created divorce and made it into a law that He gave Moses:

Wherefore they are no more twain, but one flesh. What therefore God hath joined together, let not man put asunder. They say unto him, Why did Moses then command to give a writing of divorcement, and to put her away? He saith unto them, Moses because of the hardness of your hearts suffered you to put away your wives: but from the beginning it was not so. - Matthew 19: 6-8

However, God wants marriages to be successful. He also wants them to be peaceful and happy. Here again, hardened hearts makes this impossible. He expects us to iron out our differences and work things out in a sensible way. In the case of abuse, lives can be at stake and it would be stupid to remain in the presence of someone that wants to cause us harm. He gave us common sense to run from danger. That's why our bodies are equipped with alarm buttons that let our brains know when a life threatening

situation is about to happen. It tells us to RUN!!

In the case of an abusive relationship, I feel that divorce should be the last option if the abuser refuses to change. They would have to realize that what they are doing is wrong and get their life squared up with the Lord. They would have to prove this change in their actions to their spouse in order to make their relationship work out.

Abusive relationships can be turned around into something good.

This takes the help of God and for a couple to surrender to Him. This would involve removing the things in their life that may be causing them to abuse others (such as drugs, alcohol, stress, etc). It may also take going to counseling or seeking medical help.

There are success stories out there of people who have suffered from abuse and is now living happily ever after with their spouse. That means there is hope.

Sex

God invented sex. It's great for making babies. The world is overpopulated today because a lot of people are doing it. Animals, in the water and on land, are doing it. Let's face it! It's great recreational fun and a wonderful pass time for husbands and wives all over the world. It's better than baseball, fishing and hunting! It relieves stress and tension. That makes it great for our health, too. So why is sex one of the top reasons for divorce?

Here are the problems with sex in the marriage:

No Sex
Too Little Sex
Too Much Sex
Sex With The Wrong Person
(Adultery)

For the most part, it's a quantity issue. It seems that some people in a marriage think of sex as a bad thing and don't want it at all or very little. Some think that sex is entirely what the marriage is all about and want it 24/7. If they can't get it, they'll find it elsewhere. They're all wrong. Marriage is about love and sex is the spiritual topping on the marriage cake. It adds the flavor of sweetness and makes it worth taking a bite into.

Here's a some poetic words from the Bible about sex and marriage:

Drink waters out of thine own cistern, and running waters out of thine own well. Let thy fountains be dispersed abroad, and rivers of waters in the streets. Let them be only thine own, and not strangers' with thee. Let thy fountain be blessed: and rejoice with the wife of thy youth. Let her be as the loving hind and pleasant roe; let her breasts satisfy thee at all times; and be thou ravished always with her love. - Proverbs 5: 15-19

Even according to the Bible, sex and marriage go great together.

The waters and river flowing in the streets, as mentioned in these verses, is the outward appearance to the world of how awesome the marriage relationship is. It then becomes a reflection of God and His perfectness.

Here's the deal. We are all born with natural sexual desires. We were all born with them. You, me, them... everybody! The problems happen when these desires get out of control.

Now concerning the things whereof ye wrote unto me: It is good for a man not to touch a woman. Nevertheless, to avoid fornication, let every man have his own wife, and let every woman have her own husband. Let the husband render unto the wife due benevolence: and likewise also the wife unto the husband. The wife hath not power of her own body, but the husband: and likewise also the husband hath not power of his own body, but the wife. Defraud ye not one the other, except it be with consent for a time, that ye may give yourselves to fasting and prayer; and come together again, that Satan tempt you not for your. - 1 Corinthians 7: 1-5

The word 'benevolence' means 'gift'. The word 'incontinency' means 'failure to restrain sexual appetite'. Sex in the marriage becomes a weapon to fight against losing control of our natural sexual desires. As a married couple, we should give our spouse the sexual ammunition to fight against it. If we neglect them in the bedroom, we're basically putting them out on the battlefield without a weapon. They could become a victim of temptation that could eventually destroy them and their marriage.

Since we all know now that we have natural sexual desires, we may not want to add anything to our life that will make these desires too overwhelming. Things such as pornography and X-rated movies would be unhealthy for the relationship. This could be the reason why wanting 'too much sex' in the relationship becomes an issue. The person craves sex only because of what they've allowed themselves to see. Their spouse then becomes used as a tool for relief. And nobody wants to be used.

For the person in the relationship that doesn't want sex or only wants it on rare occasions, there may be some mental or emotional issues going on. Maybe this person was a victim of a sexual sin that was committed on them as a child. They may see sex as the last thing they need in their life. The very act of natural sex with their spouse may bring back memories of a bad past. This will take sympathy, patience and understanding from their partner. They will have to talk about this problem together. And with the Lord's help, they can overcome it.

Sex in a marriage is a gift from God and was intended to be a good thing. It should strengthen the marriage and help the relationship grow. If both people could learn more about each other, become more understanding of each others needs and give of themselves, sex in the marriage would never be a problem. Divorce would never be an option.

Addictions

Addiction is defined as the state of being enslaved to a habit or practice or to something that is psychologically or physically habit-forming to such an extent that its difficult to stop. That's a long definition and you might have to read it again to get the full effect of it. I know I did.

There are several types of addictions out there. Here are a few of them:

Drug and alcohol addictions
Work addictions
Gambling addictions
Other psychological addictions

Being married to someone with an addiction can cause a lot of stress in the marriage. It can create financial problems, communication issues and separation from the family. It may seem that the best solution to the overall problem is to get a divorce. It's their problem, not yours, right? Well, maybe not.

You married this person for better and for worse. Having to deal with an addict would then fall into the 'worse' category. Unless, of course, you're the victim of physical or mental abuse. No one should have to be in a situation like that.

You married this person and made a vow to be with them during the bad times. As a loving spouse, you can actually help them. They need you.

The first step to their recovery is for them to realize that they have a problem. Many addicts don't even know they have one. When the time is appropriate (like when they're sober or when you have time alone), let them know what their addiction problem is doing to the marriage. Tell them how you feel. Give them details and examples. Do this in a sincere way and don't nag them about it.

"Honey, you've been working 7 days a week for the past few months. Could you take some time off this week or try to come home earlier? We would like to spend more time with you. The kids and I love you and would like to start doing things together as a family like we used to do."

"It bothers me that I had to cancel our plans last night because you were too drunk."

The addict has to first realize they have a problem. Otherwise, they will just feel like everyone is picking on them. This makes them angry, depressed and could make them dig deeper into their addiction. But, when they see the problem, they can then start taking the steps to recovery, They will need a support group. This will include you.

All things are lawful unto me, but all things are not expedient: all things are lawful for me, but I will not be brought under the power of any. - 1 Corinthians 6: 12

The addict will have to see that the thing they are addicted to has power over them. They are controlled by it. Knowing this, can bring out our natural rebellious attitude. This can be used in a positive way because nobody wants to be controlled. An addict can then see this thing as an enemy in their life. All they need now is the strength to fight it. This is where family support, professional help, prayer and God is desperately needed.

Several years ago, I had a drinking problem. At first, I didn't think there was an issue. I enjoyed drinking and it also helped me cope with some stressful issues I had going on at the time. But, because of my wife's strength and the way she confronted me about it, I listened and realized that my drinking separated me from my family. I couldn't be a father and a husband that my family desperately needed. It was this bottle in my hand that separated us.

Knowing that was all it took to finally put that bottle down. And making that small step saved our marriage. It wasn't easy, but through prayer and having a wife that loved me helped tremendously.

There hath no temptation taken you but such as is common to man: but God is faithful, who will not suffer you to be tempted above that ye are able; but will with the temptation also make a way to escape, that ye may be able to bear it. - 1 Corinthians 10: 13

There are many support groups out there that can help people suffering from addiction. Get plugged in, but don't let them go at it alone. Go with them and do it together as a team. You could gain some helpful knowledge that you can use to help them at home. Plus, the simple thing as working together will also strengthen your love for each other and the marriage.

Recovering from an addiction will take time, patience and the both of you will have to fight many battles together during the process. The strength of the marriage will be tested. It's best to include God in the recovery plan because the both of you will need Him.

People Change

"She was so beautiful on our wedding day. She was always the quiet and shy type. She had the ability to speak to me with her loving eyes. She was so perfect. But, five years later, all she does is nag me to death. I'm completely miserable. This is NOT the person I married. She changed!"

"He had that certain look to him. His hair was combed so neatly, face shaved smooth and he smelled so good. I was the luckiest girl alive. I had finally found Prince Charming! But then something happened after we got married. All he does now is sit in front of that TV! He's gotten fat and scraggly-looking and smells like a brewery! He's gross! I can't even stand to look at him. What happened? This is NOT the man I married. He changed!"

Many married couples today find themselves in this situation. The spouse that they currently live with isn't the same person they fell in love with and married many years ago. Because of this new change in their true love, a person may be reconsidering their commitment to the relationship. Some have chosen divorce.

It's like ordering some sweet tea at a restaurant and the waitress brings you unsweetened tea. It looks the same, but when you taste it, the first thing you want to do is spit it out. But, the fact of the matter is, it's still tea. Yes, you could create a ruckus and give it back and get another one. Or maybe you could just simply add some sugar to it.

Here again is another example of the 'for better or for worse' section of the vow you made on your wedding day. You agreed to love and cherish them even in the bad times. This doesn't mean you have to accept this new change. If you truly love each other and honor your vows, you can work together

and turn this thing into something positive.

Talk About It

As a married team, it's a good idea to talk about your problems with one another. Sometimes people don't realize they have a problem until someone says something. If your spouse loves you, they will listen to what you have to say. Let them know how their new lifestyle affects you and the marriage. Listen to their side of the story and come up with a solution together. The worse thing you can do is be negative towards them. This usually turns into arguments.

Let no corrupt communication proceed out of your mouth, but that which is good to the use of edifying, that it may minister grace unto the hearers. - Ephesians 4: 29

I used to wear 'holy' blue jeans. It wasn't because a priest sprinkled water on them. It was basically a pair of jeans that had holes in the leg. I wore them because they were comfortable. The holes allowed air to come in and cool my knee caps during hot Summer days. I loved them. However, my wife hated them and I didn't understand why.

I would always wear them in public and not think twice about it. My wife had to re-teach me on how to properly dress in public. I learned through her lesson plan that wearing 'holy' jeans gave the impression that I was a bum. I never knew that before, so together we tossed those jeans in the garbage. Problem solved.

Work At It

People don't change overnight. We shouldn't expect them to. However, if they are willing to change, we should be willing to help them as much as we can to achieve the goal. We help them because we love them and the ultimate goal will be something that will benefit the both of us.

Two are better than one; because they have a good reward for their labour. For if they fall, the one will lift up his fellow: but woe to him that is alone when he falleth; for he hath not another to help him up. Again, if two lie together, then they have heat: but how can one be warm alone? And if one prevail against him, two shall withstand him; and a threefold cord is not quickly broken. - Ecclesiastes 4: 9-12

Adding God to the team and prayer would help things flow much better. He becomes that third 'twine' in the 'marriage rope' that helps hold it all together.

Be Patient

As with all problems in a marriage, fixing them together takes time and patience. Helping someone change won't be easy.

Charity suffereth long, and is kind – 1 Corinthians 13: 4a

Because you love them, you will be willing to stick with the program for the long haul. As long as they are working towards the goal, sacrificially suffer with them during the process.

Trying To Change People

What if the problem isn't that the spouse has changed? What if they are still the same person they were on the day they got married? What if the real problem is that their spouse is trying to change them into something different? This happens.

If they married someone for who they are, why would they expect them to be any different 5, 10 or 20 years from now? They shouldn't. Maybe the solution is for them to focus on themselves.

And why beholdest thou the mote that is in thy brother's eye, but considerest not the beam that is in thine own eye? Or how wilt thou say to thy brother, Let me pull out the mote out of thine eye; and, behold, a beam is in thine own eye? - Matthew 7: 3, 4

They could start by asking themselves:

- Have I changed?
- Am I the same person I was back then?
- What changes have I made?

By changing the chemistry composition of how the marriage began, there could be conflicts. It may be a great idea to put it all back together like it used to be, even if it means making some personal changes to ourselves.

Change Can Be A Good Thing
Let's say a couple gets together. They love each other and see they were made for one another. They enjoy the same things in life and their relationship is perfect, so they get married. Everything is great!

For years into the marriage, the couple does everything together. Basically, doing what any young wild couple does in a world that's wide open to explore.

Then one day, the fun stops. The other spouse no longer wants to do those things they used to do. Instead, they are reading the Bible and going to church. They're praying and praising God. They begin removing things in their life that now they say they no longer need. They're talking and acting differently. I mean, it's not a bad thing but it's definitely different. What's going on?

This person has given their life to Jesus and now it seems like their spouse is left out in the cold. Spiritually, it's great that this person has made preparations for eternity, but physically, it has caused some changes in the marriage with positive results.

Maybe this new lifestyle is worth checking into?

The best thing that could happen in a relationship like this is if both of them could serve the Lord together. Because the Bible says, "God is love", it could only grow their love even more and give them a stronger foundation to stand upon.

No Time Together

Time is one of the precious things we have in life and it flies by so quickly. A day has 24 hours in it, and on the average, 8 hours of that is spent sleeping. That leaves 16 hours available for use every day. How does a person spend his 'waking' hours?

Most people work at a job that requires at least 8 hours of their time plus maybe an hour to travel back and forth. Now we're left with 7 hours to use how we want during the week with 32 hours available on the weekends. And when you add all of that up, that gives us a grand total of 67 hours available for the entire week. Wow!

With so many available hours, why do couples feel that their spouse doesn't spend time with them? It's a serious problem that has become a reason for divorce.

There are so many distractions

in the world today that tries to consume our time. We have a lot of things to do, to look at, to learn about and people to socialize with. However, our spouses end up being the last ones on the list.

We have to prioritize the important things in life:

1. **God**
2. **Our Spouse**
3. **Our Kids**
4. **Money and Other Stuff**

This doesn't mean we have to multi-task to fit them all in at the same time, but to actually stop what we are doing and spend time with each one individually. It's important for building and growing relationships.

So teach us to number our days, that we may apply our hearts unto wisdom. - Psalms 90: 12

For people out there that are considering divorce because their spouse doesn't spend time with them, there is hope. The first step is to let them know that there is an issue that's affecting the marriage. Communication is the key! If there's true love in the relationship, then both of them will listen to each other.

Next, they should evaluate how their time is spent throughout the day. Write it down. They may see that a lot of time is being wasted when it could be used for something more constructive. Set priorities and adjust the schedule accordingly by giving each item on the list a time slot in their busy day.

For which of you, intending to build a tower, sitteth not down first, and counteth the cost, whether he have sufficient to finish it? - Luke 14: 28

It's all about planning and making time to be with the ones you love. When you do, the love relationship can grow. Marriages become healthier and happier.

Remember the sabbath day, to keep it holy. Six days shalt thou labour, and do all thy work: But the seventh day is the sabbath of the LORD thy God: in it thou shalt not do any work, thou, nor thy son, nor thy daughter, thy manservant, nor thy maidservant, nor thy cattle, nor thy stranger that is within thy gates: For in six days the LORD made heaven and earth, the sea, and all that in them is, and rested the seventh day: wherefore the LORD blessed the sabbath day, and hallowed it. - Exodus 20: 8-11

And remember, according to God's plan, one day a week should be used for resting and spending time with Him. He should be our number one priority on our list. This can be done as a family and can be a great way to get the family together. Put everybody in the minivan and go to church somewhere.

Jealousy/Insecurity

A man and woman get together and decide to get married. They're in love and everything seems to flow like butter. That is until one of them begins talking to one of their friends who happens to be of the opposite sex. Seems harmless, right? But, not to their spouse. That's because jealousy kicked in.

"So, who were you talking to?"

"Aww, an old friend from school. We've been friends since we were kids."

"It didn't look like a friendly conversation to me. Both of you were smiling and making eyes at each other."

"Oh no. He's a great guy. I haven't seen him in a long time. It sure was good talking about old memories."

"I'm sure it was. From the way it looked, it appeared to be more than friendly chatter."

"Say what? You think I'm cheating on you?"

"Well, that's how it looked to me. Friends don't smile at each other or make eyes at one another."

"Smiles?!! Eyes?!! What are you talking about??!!"

"I just call it the way I see it."

"OH, NO!! YOU AIN'T GOING THERE!! LET ME TELL YOU A THING OR TWO...!!"

Needless to say, this led into a big argument over a friendly conversation between two friends. Mean words were said back and forth. Fortunately for them, love stepped in and saved their marriage. They were able to talk it out and settle their differences.

Many married couples today can't say that about their marriage. They let things blowup and the only option to them seems to be divorce. That's sad to me because many times these things can be worked out.

What is the root of the problem? Pretty simple – it's jealousy and insecurity. They're the dynamic duo that

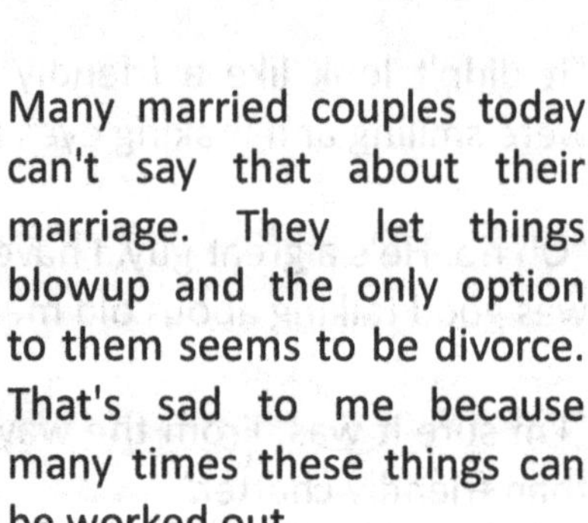

hops into the marriage scene and tries to drive everyone insane. They poke and stir up trouble and find our weak spots. They're ugly!

Let's take a closer look at them individually. Maybe we can see why they're such a terrible enemy to a relationship:

Jealousy

Jealousy is an emotion that can manifest itself in a number of interpersonal relationships - romantic or not. It originates in a feeling that someone else has an advantage that you don't or that a person dear to you favors someone else over you.

There is no fear in love; but perfect love casteth out fear: because fear hath torment. He that feareth is not made perfect in love. - 1 John 4: 18

But let every man prove his own work, and then shall he have rejoicing in himself alone, and not in another. For every man shall bear his own burden. - Galatians 6: 4, 5

We shouldn't feel like we have to be competitive in marriage, nor should we fear that our spouse is having another relationship with someone else behind our backs, especially when there's no proof.

In some cases, the real proof is right there in front of our faces. We may have caught them in the act or have seen the evidence lying around. Jealousy then would be a normal response, but the problem is in the love relationship. It's not true love and it's something that needs to be discussed between the married couple. There could be several reasons for why the 'cheating' is going on – it could be lust or that the 'cheating spouse' is missing something from the marriage relationship. The key here is to talk about it and get to the root of the problem. From there, you can work together to resolve it as a team.

Insecurity

Insecurity is having a lack of confidence or assurance.

Be careful for nothing; but in every thing by prayer and supplication with thanksgiving let your requests be made known unto God. And the peace of God, which passeth all understanding, shall keep your hearts and minds through Christ Jesus. Finally, brethren, whatsoever things are true, whatsoever things are honest, whatsoever things are just, whatsoever things are pure, whatsoever things are lovely, whatsoever things are of good report; if there be any virtue, and if there be any praise, think on these things. Those things, which ye have both learned, and received, and heard, and seen in me, do: and the God of peace shall be with you. - Philippians 4: 6-9

The feeling of insecurity can put a strain on a marriage. Those feelings of fear and anxiety can cause torment in a person that will eventually affect both spouses. A person suffering from insecurity may feel that they are unworthy or that they could never measure up to what their spouse may expect. It's a battle that goes on in their mind. It's awful. Then there's the what if's:

- What if I can't make my spouse happy?
- What if they find someone better than me?

- What if I get old and wrinkly, will they still hang around?

In order to protect their mental state, they become possessive and paranoid. This leads into things such as monitoring their spouse's phone calls and emails, wanting to know where they've been and what they did while they were out and about. This could go into more extremes such as not letting them leave the house so that they can be monitored 24/7. This is not a relationship that anyone would want to be in.

God wants our marriage relationships to be peaceful and happy. We have to trust and communicate with the ones we love. If a trust has been broken in the past, work together to get it fixed in the present so that you can move forward together into the future.

Kids

How in the world can those cute little people we created cause problems in a marriage? I mean, they're so cute and carry some of our traits. They're like little 'mini-me's' crawling or walking around the house. I mean, we know they create worries, make us tired and cost us a fortune. But, they can cause divorce, too? Wow! Let's look into this a little bit more.

Many married couples will say that their happiest times were before they had kids. It's not that they didn't love them, but somewhere between delivering them at the hospital to the present day, something changed in the relationship. The couple argues more, they smile less and many times it has something to do with the kids they put into this world. What's the deal?

I can see how marriages can be happy when there are just two people involved. There are only two people that you have to be concerned about. All you have to do is please them and yourself. That's fairly easy, right? Then, all of a sudden, a baby is born and parents are created.

At first this little thing is cute and both parents are excited and everything is so sweet. Birds are chirping and heavenly harps are playing and then a stink enters the room. It's now time for the first diaper change. Since the little fella can't change himself yet, it's up to one of the parents. Whose job is it? Well, the couple's not really sure yet. That's when the arguments begin.

'Whose job is it?' seems to be the root of the problem when it comes to kids. Working out a plan early in the game on 'who does what' will help later on in life. For couples that don't discuss their parenting roles, they may end up calling it quits. They give up in the form of divorce papers and lawyer's fees.

Trying To Parent Our Kids

Lo, children are an heritage of the LORD: and the fruit of the womb is his reward. - Psalms 127: 3

Kids are a gift from God. The Bible says it and I believe it, too. I am blessed because I have a few of them floating around out there. And regardless of how goofy they act sometimes, I am fulfilled in my heart knowing that they are my children. They can't help the way they act because that's a genetic trait they got from their mother. They just can't help it. Bless their heart.

Having kids is great, but it would've been good if they came with an instruction book on 'how to raise them' because parenting is a hard job. It requires the help of both parents in order to have healthy family relationships. There are things that each parent contributes that helps the kid grow and become able to survive out there in this crazy mixed up world.

That doesn't mean that kids raised by two parents automatically turn out to be outstanding citizens. Nor does it mean that a kid with only one parent will turn out to be scum. Actually, there are a bunch of kids out there that have turned out fine with only one parent raising them. I should know because I am one of them. God has mercy for kids like us and will put the proper people in our life to fill in those gaps.

A father of the fatherless, and a judge of the widows, is God in his holy habitation. - Psalms 68: 5

Having two parents simply makes the whole parenting job much easier when the work is equally distributed. Without it, problems happen, arguments are started and marriages get stressed.

Some folks believe that it's the woman's job to raise the kids. They feel that the men are to jump into the parenting role only after the woman has done everything she can. This isn't how it's supposed to be. It takes two. Fathers and mothers are equally important.

And, ye fathers, provoke not your children to wrath: but bring them up in the nurture and admonition of the Lord. - Ephesians 6: 4

Raising kids together under the guidance of the Lord makes perfect sense. As He works in our life to become more like Jesus, He is also training us to become better parents. This creates in us the moral values and traits of good role models for the next generation. As parents, we need to work together with our spouses in helping our kids grow. This takes communication, teamwork and love for each other.

Trying To Please Our Kids

From the moment our kids were born, we began catering to their needs. Their cries became a ringing bell that told us when our help was desperately needed. We were always quick to respond to the call.

I can remember the many nights being asleep in my bed and hearing the loud screams of our babies coming from their bedroom. It's probably the worst sound you would want to hear knowing you had to work the next day. I also remember my wife waking up in the wee hours of the morning to check on them. Most of the time all they needed was a bottle and a diaper change. She would always meet their needs.

As parents, this doesn't stop when they are babies. We carry this '911 parenting trait' on to their toddler years all the way through to their teenage years.

I can't count the numerous times my kids would say they needed something, especially when we're out shopping.

"Mom, I gotta have this shirt."

"Buy me these shoes. I need them."

Most of the time, they already had one like it in their closet at home. It seems we always try to meet their needs whether it's legitimate or not.

And for some of us, even though our kids are moved out and married, we're 'still on duty'. All it takes is a phone call. We're there! It seems parenting never ends and we're always trying to please them.

To some, this may not be a problem. They love it when their kids call out to them for help. They are quick to reach out with a helping hand. The problems happen when we neglect our spouse by always putting our kid's needs and wants to the top of our priority list. The time that we should be spending with our marriage partner is now used on them. This creates marital issues and can lead to divorce.

We have to make time to be with the one we married. Without it, the marriage will suffer. We also have to work together as a married team to raise our child. When our child requires our attention, we need to analyze the need to make sure it's a real one. Believe it or not, there are kids out there that are spoiled rotten and will consume your whole day if you let them. We have to set priorities and boundaries. In some cases, what that kid needs is some discipline.

He that spareth his rod

hateth his son: but he that loveth him chasteneth him betimes. - Proverbs 13: 24
Withhold not correction from the child: for if thou beatest him with the rod, he shall not die. - Proverbs 23: 13

The rod and reproof give wisdom: but a child left to himself bringeth his mother to shame. Correct thy son, and he shall give thee rest; yea, he shall give delight unto thy soul. - Proverbs 29: 15, 17

When a child is old enough to handle their own problems, it's best as a parent to let them work it out. It develops character and strengthens them as a person in the process.

Train up a child in the way he should go: and when he is old, he will not depart from it. - Proverbs 22: 6

If you're constantly catering to a child all the time, not only does

it put a strain on your marriage, it also develops children who will grow up to become adults that won't know how to survive in the world on their own. They will end up being a 40-year old that's still living with their parents and sleeping on their couch. And that's not a good thing! According to Proverbs 22: 6, we are to train them in the way they should GO. That means that the ultimate goal is to get them out of your house. Just

sayin'.

Kid's Rank On The Priority List

We're back to the priority list for our marriage:

1. God
2. Our Spouse
3. **Our Kids**
4. Money and Other Stuff

You will notice that 'kids' rank in third place in our marriage relationship. We have to keep God and our spouse at the top because, in a few short years, the kids will be gone and these two will be what you have left. It's best to keep the relationship with them as strong as possible during the parenting process. If it's done correctly, the kids won't suffer. Actually they will be better people because of it and will learn from you. They will have better marriages and they will carry this 'training' on to their children. Your dedication will save marriages for many generations to come.

Livin' Happily Ever After

Livin' Happily Ever After

Marriage is a great thing regardless of what other people say. It could be that they don't know about the happy and peaceful parts that come from having a healthy relationship.

Yes, there will be bumpy roads along the way, but true love will keep a married couple on the right course. Even though there will be disagreements and issues, a couple that loves one another will make every effort to resolve them together.

In a healthy relationship, this true love that a couple has for one another in the beginning will continue to grow more and more each day. It will keep them driving onward towards 'happily ever after'.

You're probably thinking, "Happily ever after? Yeah, right! That stuff only happens in fairy tales!"

But, it is possible. Keep in mind, marriage was God's idea. He created it and blessed it. He doesn't make crap. His stuff is perfect, and based on history, it's usually man that messes everything up.

So God created man in his own image, in the image of God

created he him; male and female created he them. And God blessed them, and God said unto them, Be fruitful, and multiply, and replenish the earth, and subdue it: - Genesis 1: 27, 28a

He had a perfect plan for mankind — be fruitful and multiply. He didn't want us to do it all alone. He created someone to fill that emptiness in our hearts. He put man and woman together.

And the LORD God said, It is not good that the man should be alone; I will make him an help meet for him. - Genesis 2: 18

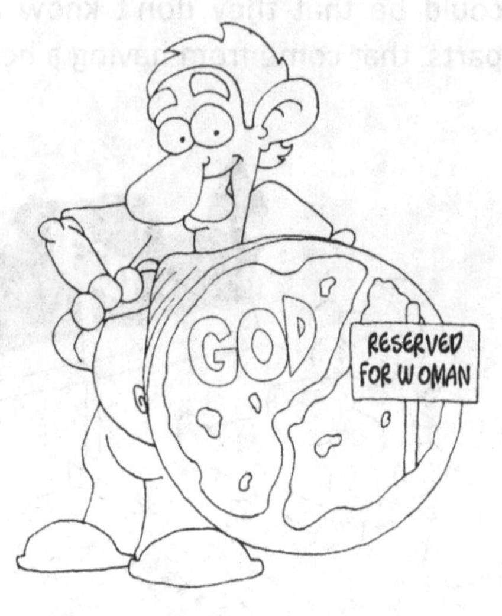

In this relationship ordained by God, we become one with them. This is why we get married.

Therefore shall a man leave his father and his mother, and shall cleave unto his wife: and they shall be one flesh. - Genesis 2: 24

Marriage is a good thing. Since it came from God, the plan for a successful marriage would also come from Him, too. That's what the Bible is for. It's a road map! We have to actually read it to know where we're going.

We also have to surrender to God's plan for us – both individually and as a married couple. This would mean allowing Him to be the foundation that our marriage sits upon. This is how you reach 'happily ever after' because God will take you there if you let Him.

The alternative is divorce. Divorce is such an ugly word and wasn't part of the original plan. But because of man's hardened hearts in the days of Moses, God invented it. And it comes with some bad side effects.

Divorce - It's Effect On Kids

You would think that getting divorced only affects the couple that is wanting to do it, but that's not always true. It can also affect their friends, their families, and especially their children.

Married couples that have chosen to divorce should consider their kid's thoughts and emotions about it. Believe it or not, they're in it, too.

Here's what I found out about how divorce affects our children:

Insecure and afraid of the future
There are a lot of changes that goes on in divorce. This could affect a child's sense of security and make them worry about their future. The 'what next?' questions stir around in their minds:

- Will we be poor?
- Will we have enough to eat?
- Will I have to go to a new school?
- Will I still see my friends?

These and among other thoughts create worries in our children.

Fear of being abandoned
In divorce, a child no longer has one of his/her parents living at

home. They may feel that the other parent will leave them, too. This change was sudden and scary. They may not know what to expect next.

Rejected and to blame
A child may take the blame for the divorce and feel that it was their fault that their parents are no longer together. Or they may feel that one of the parents no longer love them.

Powerless
A child may try everything in their power to try and get their parents back together. When they fail, they may feel powerless and helpless.

Torn in two
When parents argue, a child may suffer emotional trauma because they may feel expected to take sides. They could feel trapped in a 'no-win' situation.

Sad
Divorce is a sad moment for a child. They could feel a huge sense of loss – very similar to a death of a parent. If left unmanaged, this could lead to depression.

Stressed
Divorce can put a strain on a child. They may feel like they have to 'grow up' quickly so that they can be the referee between their parents. This 'big job' can create stress.

Lonely
Keep in mind, divorce means that the child will only live with one parent at a time. They may miss the relationship of having both parents together. Without it, it could leave them feeling lonely. They could try to cope with this feeling elsewhere or become

withdrawn.

Angry

Kids may not understand divorce or accept it. This could create anger and resentment.

Depressed

Depression can set in with the child. This is normally considered a 'second stage' emotion. It is usually linked to any or all of the above. They will need support to help deal with all of these emotions percolating inside of them..

Divorce is rough on everyone involved. It is best to think about this important step more in depth before actually going through with it. Make every effort to fix the marriage as a team and consider divorce as a last resort, especially when kids are involved.

Divorce - It's Effect
On Future Relationships

The way many people think of marriage is that a person in the relationship can be replaced. If you get tired of them or the marriage doesn't work out, you can always go out and try again. Instead of considering the 'holy union' it was meant to be, we think of it more in terms of a cheap product – if it breaks or wears out, get a another one.

No big deal, right?

I was amazed at what I found about 2nd and 3rd marriages. If a 1st marriage has a 50% failure rate, the stats for 2nd and 3rd marriages are even worse:

60% of 2nd marriages end in divorce
70% of 3rd marriages end in divorce

Why does the failure rate increase? You would think that things should get better the 2nd time around and especially the 3rd. So, what's the problem?

The main reason is called 'baggage'. Because this is a new relationship that is replacing a previous one, there will be 'baggage' brought over. This is like the 'leftovers' that were created from the first marriage. It can include children, ex-spouses and even the problems that caused the first divorce to begin with. All of these things will have to be dealt with in order for the second relationship to even work out.

The Kids
For relationships that involve children, there will be conflicts. The new husband or wife wants to be the number one priority in their spouse's life. However, this spouse has children that want to be their parent's first priority. The battle begins and the husband or wife will have to make a serious decision. The correct answer is to put their new spouse at the top of the list. But, many aren't willing to do it. This leads to arguments and, in some cases, a divorce happens.

Plus, trying to parent kids that don't biologically belong to you is tough to do. It's a struggle because you may feel like you have certain guidelines to follow. This isn't a good position to be in and can create marital problems unless the couple deals with it in the beginning.

The Ex
The ex-spouse never really goes away, especially when kids are involved. There's this new thing called 'child support'. It's a financial obligation that a parent must pay to the previous spouse

and parent of their child. Even though the child doesn't live with them permanently, they are required by law to help support them.

The problem is that the ex-spouse may be greedy and angry about the previous relationship. They will use the child as a leverage to get what they can from their ex. It becomes an act of revenge. This affects the second relationship because the new spouse is stuck in the middle in this money war. It gets ugly sometimes.

Previous Marriage Problems

The first step a person should take in a second marriage is to figure out why the first one failed. The solution would be to not make the same mistakes again, even if you're part of the problem.

Many times people tend to put all the blame on their ex and think all they have to do is find Mr/Mrs Right. But, the fact is, no one is perfect. A marriage relationship requires work from both people and may involve some self improvement for it all to work out. If we are truly honest with ourselves and discover our faults in the previous marriage, it would be a good idea to correct them before entering the new one. If not, the same problems will happen again.

Another issue in second marriages is that people bring the scars of the previous marriage into the new one. A person may stay in 'defense mode' all the time because they may be afraid of being hurt again. This causes trust issues in this new relationship. It's hard to have a healthy marriage without trust. It just doesn't work.

Many times people involved in second marriages develop a 'been there, done that... ain't doing it again' mentality. If problems occur in the new marriage that simulates the old one, a couple is less likely to forgive and put up with it. They are 'quick to the draw' when it comes to divorce because they won't tolerate reliving something that they have already been through.

All of these reasons could be why many 2nd and 3rd marriages don't work out. However, there are some that do. It could be that they set priorities, communicate and apply the lessons they learned from the first marriage to the new one. Yes, divorce can affect new relationships. But, it's our choice whether we use it in a positive or negative way.

'til Death Do Us Part

Healthy Marriages – Sources Of Info

You can read about how to maintain healthy marriages just about anywhere. It's on the Internet and there are books in every bookstore all over the world. But, the fact is, everyone has their own idea of how it should work and sometimes their advice doesn't help.

The Bible, to me, is the best source because it's written to us from the Creator Himself. He made us and He knows how to keep everything together – this includes marriages. Using His awesome instruction manual for our life wouldn't be a bad idea.

Another great source of information on how to live 'happily ever after' with the ones we love would be to ask people that know from experience. It's those couples out there that are living proof that marriages can stay together for many years. Ask someone you know.

I recently asked my friends on Facebook, "What is the secret to a long lasting marriage?" Here's what they had to say:

"Definitely communication and time alone with just the two of you. Try to remember what drew you to each other in the first place and keep things fresh. Don't get caught up in routines, you'll forget to appreciate what the other has to offer." - T. Callaway

"Once upon a time, I was told never to go to bed angry. But if both of you are so bull-headed, it doesn't always work out." - D. Tollerson

"If you're having a heated discussion and it's going nowhere, take a 30-minute break from each other so you can discuss it in a calm and rational way without screaming at each other. It's so much easier to hear if no one is shouting." - S. Price

"Always remember to have fun together. And when you get really frustrated with each other, think about why you fell in love to start with. Never stop kissing and holding hands." - A. Knott

"After 30 years, I can tell you... there is no secret. The most important thing I've learned is that you have to take the vow, "for better or worse", seriously. It's not all champagne and roses, no matter how compatible you think you are." - B. Bruhn

"It's about loving family and most of all trust... so you can be there for each other." - S. Houze

"I've only been married a little over ten years, but I already know a few keys to stayin' married: 1. Never go to bed angry. 2. Think about how little time we actually have with each other. 3. Don't be selfish. 4. Make sure you marry for the right reasons in the first place. 5. Do the dishes." - G. Johnson

"Communication is the true key and at the heart of it all... without it, words are not spoken and assumptions are made - making distance." - J. Sabine

"Share everything with each other, except shoes and toilet paper." - M. Brock

"Find things that you both enjoy and do them together. I like to travel. He learned to love it with me. He likes to yard sale. I learned to love it, too. Have an open mind and love each other enough to give new things a try. Seeing the joy it brings THEM is sometimes enough to make YOU happy." - D. Rooks

"ALWAYS PUT JESUS FIRST IN YOUR MARRIAGE! If both of you believe the Word of God and you study the Bible together, pray together. God will make a way when there seems to be no way! God is good and He needs to be answering your questions in life. He also needs to be making your decisions as well." - B. Hooten

"Love is a choice. You choose to stay in love even when you don't feel it. And there are times you won't. It's those times that the power of forgiveness can make you or break you. You have to forgive or bitterness creeps in and can and will destroy you. You have to remember you are two different people with two ways of seeing things. Communicate. Forgive. Commitment." - C. Craft

"We've been married for 23 years. Laughter....don't forget to laugh. My husband said he gave up being a gymnast and going to the Olympics for me. I don't think he can touch his toes. Haha! Choose your words. You can't take them back after they have been said!" - K. Brooks

"It isn't always about agreeing, but more about understanding. Your differences are what compliment each other. You may not always like each other, but you always love each other." - M. Crowe

"Keep Christ in the center of your marriage!" - M. Mims

"I met my hubby at 19 and got married 3 years later. We've been together for 13 years (married 10 years). Ours has always been no secrets. If we have a problem, we talk it out instead of letting it build up into an explosion. We also have taken time for us to spend time together as a couple and apart from each other." - M. McFall

"When and if you fight, don't take it personal." - J. Smith

"Learning to be selfless. I think when you are younger, you tend to be more selfish. That is why it is tough on young marriages. As you grow older, you should become more selfless in your relationships; being considerate of others before yourself. That tends to go against a world view of I and ME, so it is becoming more uncommon to find lasting relationships with a selfish mindset. It's being able to pour love out and not 'just receive' is what I think is the key." - C. Jackson

"Communication and trust. It helps if you're best friends also!" - D. Eidson

"Communication, trust, TRUE love, laugh together EVERYDAY, don't take EVERYTHING so serious all of the time and also you both have to be given your own space. Never go to bed angry, and ALWAYS ALWAYS say 'I love you' when leaving each others side or on the phone because you never know what life has in store for you in the next moment. I have been with Mark since March 7, 1984 and I still get excited when I see him pull up in the driveway at home.

That is when you know you are still in love. P.S. NEVER NEVER EVER EVER let money or money issues take your power. You have to be in love WITH money and WITHOUT it." - *K. Cochran*

"Remember that not only do you have a life together, but you also need your own time and space. It will make you happier with each other." – *K. Congo*

"Don't play the blame game with each other or keep score. Each person should give 100%." - *B. Carroll*

"Liking to do things together and letting each other do their own thing. Laughter and more laughter. Letting go of the little things and remembering that most everything is really just a little thing." - *C. Broome*

"Never marry for anything less than TRUE LOVE because that's what gets you through the hard times." - *M. Smith*

"A long, long time ago when Ken and I came to Newnan to get our marriage license, my mother or father had to sign for us to get married because I wasn't 21. After we left the court house, I asked my mother what the secret was to her marriage and why they never had a fight. This is what she told me, "When your dad gets mad, I keep my mouth shut and when I get mad he BETTER keep his shut!" Of course, I laughed until I cried, but you know what, it's the truth. When your husband or wife gets angry don't pour fuel on the fire. If one of you can remain calm, the situation doesn't blow up. Words can never be taken back once they are out of your mouth. No matter how many times you say you're sorry, the words are there and cannot be forgotten. My parents were married for well over 50 years and had 6 kids and I only know of 1 disagreement they had in all the years I was living under their roof. They loved and respected each other until the end and that is truly amazing to me. Ken and I will be married 47 years this December and we still enjoy each other. We talk to each other and laugh a lot. It boils down to mutual respect and love for each other." - *D. Mims*

"You can be right or happy, but you can't be both. And my husband taught me how to shoot. But seriously, talking to GOD a lot! - 22 yrs married." - *A. Smith*

"Just because you're mad doesn't mean you have to stay mad. Walk away. But the main key of all marriages... keep God first." - *B. Boyd*

"Mike is my soulmate. The secret to a good marriage? Keep God in your

marriage. Say 'I love you' everyday. Kiss everyday. Hug and dance often. NEVER, NEVER go to bed angry. Remember that date nights are a must and when the world seems like its falling apart around you, hold on tight and never let go. Never have secrets. Mike is my best friend. We tell each other everything. He knows the worst about me and it's OK. After 12 years of marriage, he can walk into the room and my heart still goes pitter-patter. That's when you know it's true love." - C. Robards

"LEARNING HOW TO COMPROMISE. We didn't always do it but sometimes you just have to be the one to give in." - T. Ward

"Make your spouse your number one EARTHLY reason for living. God is your top priority and your spouse comes in 2nd after God. Make your spouse's happiness more important than your own (both have to do this for it to work). And NEVER say things in anger, shut up and walk away and come back and talk when you've cooled off." - M. Fitzhenry

"Compromise, fishing together and love God! 29 years married. Also, it's better to meet someone in Church than it is in a bar. Just sayin'."- K. Bright

"Forgiveness....lots of forgiveness. Let things that don't matter go." - C. Surrett

"37 years - Give each other a lot of space, trust, respect, no nagging or blaming and communicate. Lot of things change over the years. Treat each day like your first. Do not break the bond. Share." - V. Waligora

"Keep it fun, even when times are hard. Cheryl said all of the nice things above and it's all true mutually! Giving each other trust and space helps, too. I taught her how to shoot, so I'm extra nice now...LOL" – M. Robards

"Cooperation, patience, kindness, and most of all love." - J. Hill

"Giving and receiving, even if your wife is always right." - W. Gann

"43 years here! #1... NEVER go to bed mad! And a lot of people say a marriage is 50/50, but it's not...it is 100/100. You got to each give 100% of every thing." - B. Hayes

"Being joined together BY GOD & becoming ONE. Keeping GOD 1st in ALL you do. I agree with Chris. You have to take self out of the picture. Communication, loving & trusting are also key components. One thing that I have personally

learned is that you have to be there for one another regardless of the situation. God did not promise us a peaceful life - so yes we will have our valleys, but it is HOW YOU CHOOSE TO CLIMB OUT OF THAT VALLEY TO REACH THE MOUNTAIN TOP. Will you be solo? Or will you be joined together as ONE and get the job done? 12-31-12 will be 24 years for me and Billy and I must say, I fall in love with him more and more every day." - M. Mullenix

What Does It Mean to Be A

Christian

Written and illustrated by Jeff Todd

Introduction

The guidelines for Christian living have already been written. You can find everything you need to know right there in God's Holy Word - The Bible. It's just a matter of opening it up and reading it. The Spirit of God will reveal to you the things you need to know and give you the ability to understand them.

The purpose of this book is not to be a substitute for reading the Bible. Oh no! Everyone should read it. My hope and intentions for writing this book is that it will inspire you, as the reader, and will offer humorous illustrations to use in your walk with Christ and to put Christianity out there in an easy to understand format. Together we can learn to live our life to the fullest with happiness and joy that God intended for us to live.

First of all, being a Christian doesn't have to be boring and dull. I believe it should be energetic and alive. We are to be a light in the world that we live in and shine out to others. When a person sees the way we are, it should make them want to be that way, too.

Our lifestyle should point them to Jesus. Everything we say and do should reflect the One that saved us.

I have never considered myself to be like everyone else. The way I look at life may be different than the way others see it. Even as a young child, Christian people to me were always the suit and tie-wearing folks or the snooty ladies wearing the dresses and they acted very *'stiff necked'*. It was almost like they were afraid to smile.

I agree, it was wrong of me to segregate Christians like this, but those were the Christians I knew. As I grew older, I realized that not all Christians were like this and were actually normal people.

Being called into the ministry, I have to use what the Lord has given me. This includes the relationship I have with Jesus through His grace that saved me, His Word, and the gifts, talents, and characteristics that He gave me.

When you put that all together in a mixing bowl, you have:

I know from experience that being a Christian isn't a difficult task. It's not a series of rituals or following a magic formula. It's actually so simple that anyone could do it.

That's my purpose and focus of writing this book! I want to write something that would minister to people (no matter who they were) and possibly help them understand what being a Christian is all about.

It's got to be simple and easy to understand. I don't use BIG words when I speak, so why should I write BIG words when I am using this to reach people and lead them to Jesus. I can't! It's not how God made me!

If you're reading this today, this book is for you from a simple minded person like me. Being a Christian is awesome and it's not as weird as you may have heard. We're not crazy people! If you have never asked Jesus to come into your life, I hope and pray that you make that choice today.

If you're already a Christian, I hope this book ministers to you, too. Living the life you profess isn't as hard as you make it when you realize what it's all about. Actually it's not supposed to be hard at all. You're a Christian because you gave your life to Him. Sometimes we have to give it back to Him and let Him lead the way.

Excuse me for a moment. I'll be right back. I need to pray!

Dear Lord, I pray right now that You use these words from this book to reach people out there. I don't know who this is intended for or who will be reading this. I know that I belong to You and that You will use me for your glory. Please do so today. Thank you Jesus. Amen.

So, here it is folks!

What Does It Mean To Be A

Christian

The Starting Point: Jesus

Christian living begins with having Jesus Christ in your life. Period.

Let me say that again because it's important.

Christian living begins with having Jesus Christ in your life. This means that before you can live the life of a Christian, you have to have Jesus as your Lord and Savior in your life. He has to be the center of your life; the foundation that your life sits on. You can't live a Christian life if you're not a Christian.

No 'buts' about it!

But, I Go To Church

Going to church does not make you a Christian. It makes you a 'church-goer'. Even though you attend church every Sunday, in the morning and at night, it doesn't make you a Christian. You may be a Sunday school teacher and teach from the Bible. It doesn't make you a

Christian.

It's almost like calling yourself a fisherman without a fishing pole. Yes, you may go to the lake, but without a pole, you're just a... person that goes to the lake. You may know everything there is to know about fishing. You may know the different types of fish by the color of their fins and the number of sparkles in their eyes, but it doesn't make you a fisherman. You may have the best fishing boat on the lake, but without the pole, you are basically a boat owner. Are you with me?

But, I Have Christian Family

Just because one of your family members is a Christian doesn't make you one. I know this will be hard for people to believe, but being a Christian is not a genetic thing. It's a Jesus thing!

"My grandfather was a deacon at Flakey Biscuit Baptist Church. He was a Christian man that loved the Lord."

That's great! But, it doesn't make you one. The glitter from your Christian relative's walk doesn't magically fall off on you. It would be nice if it did, but it doesn't. Being a Christian and being saved is about a one on one relationship with Jesus Christ.

But, I Shook The Preacher's Hand Last Sunday

If *'hand shaking'* guaranteed a Christian life, then everybody that visited a church on a Sunday morning would be saved and so would every person that the preacher had come in contact with outside of the church. Think about it! Hand shaking is a greeting, not a magic salvation ticket! That's not how it works!

The Deal?

Here's the deal! A person can only become a Christian when they accept Jesus into their life and get saved. Saved? That's right! The day you realize that you are a sinner and that you are lost without a Savior is the day you have a choice of whether to be a Christian or not. The sad thing is that we are all

For all have sinned, and come short of the glory of God - Romans 3:23

sinners!

It's like a day at the lake. You jump in and realize you can't swim! Life was pretty smooth when you were playing close to the bank. But as you drifted out towards the deep part of the water, you realize that you needed a float. The same is true in life. You need to be saved or you will sink like a rock!

"That sounds all fine and dandy, but what am I being saved from?"

The answer is sin. It's those *'bad things'* in your life that goes against God and His way of life. To realize how bad sin is, you must first know who God is.

Who Is God?

God created everything. There is nothing in this world, on Earth, or in outer space that He did not create. He created the water, the air, the trees, animals, and He even created you.

The Bible tells us that He knew us before we were even born and that He knew ALL about us. That tells me He's the one that put us here. He put you here!

Before I formed thee in the belly I knew thee; and before thou camest forth out of the womb I sanctified thee, and I ordained thee a prophet unto the nations. – Jeremiah 1: 5

I believe that we are all here for a purpose - His purpose. But, we will never know this purpose until we give our lives to Him. For a God that created everything in this universe to take the time to make me, tells me I have a purpose for being here. The same is true for you! We need to find out what it is. This will involve getting to know the Creator.

Have you heard this one before?:

For whom he did foreknow, he also did predestinate to be conformed to the image of his Son, that he might be the firstborn among many brethren. – Romans 8: 29

He wants a relationship with you. Since you are here and have a purpose, you will need to get a relationship started with God. You will need to know more about Him. The Bible says God is holy and perfect - sinless. Now keep that thought in your mind for a moment and let's talk again about sin.

When you think of the sin in the world today, what comes to mind? Does murder and stealing? What about lying and foul language? There are all kinds of sin! Small ones to big ones and they all have one thing in common - they are still *'sin'*. Sin is what separates us from a relationship with God.

We live in a sinful world and we have sin in our lives. How can we make things right? The unfortunate thing is that WE can't! We need something or someone to fill in that gap. God knew this, too. So what needs to happen?

Don't worry! God already had that planned out because He loves us.

Here's what God did for us! He sent His only Son to die as a sacrifice for our sins. It sounds like a drastic measure to take but it's what was needed. Jesus, His Son, died for us so that we could live - eternally with God.

But wait! His death required something from us?

That's right! It says we have to BELIEVE in Him. Here's another scripture you may have heard:

That if thou shalt confess with thy mouth the Lord Jesus, and shalt believe in thine heart that God hath raised him from the dead, thou shalt be saved. - Romans 10:9

It sounds to me like God has provided a way out for us, but He also requires us to do something to be saved. We already know we are a bunch of sinners. Right?

We are to confess with our mouth the Lord Jesus? And believe in our heart?

Sounds too simple to be true, doesn't it?

It is and it starts with a simple prayer to God. After that, all we have to do is receive this gift of salvation. I believe God convicts our hearts that we are lost. It's like a helpless feeling you have inside that let's you know that you need Him in your life.

Are you feeling that right now? If so, let's get this thing settled. I know a lot of religious people and some Christians get 'weirded out' when you present a model prayer to the lost and ask them to repeat it. I can understand their way of thinking and I know that just repeating prayers doesn't save a person. It has to be heartfelt and sincere. The main points of your prayer has to cover knowing that you're lost without Jesus in your life, understanding that you're a sinner that's sorry for the junk you're doing, and that you are willing to turn from that junk and want Jesus to come in and take over.

That's basically it!

So, if you meet that criteria and would like to accept Jesus as your Lord and Savior, let's do this thing together.

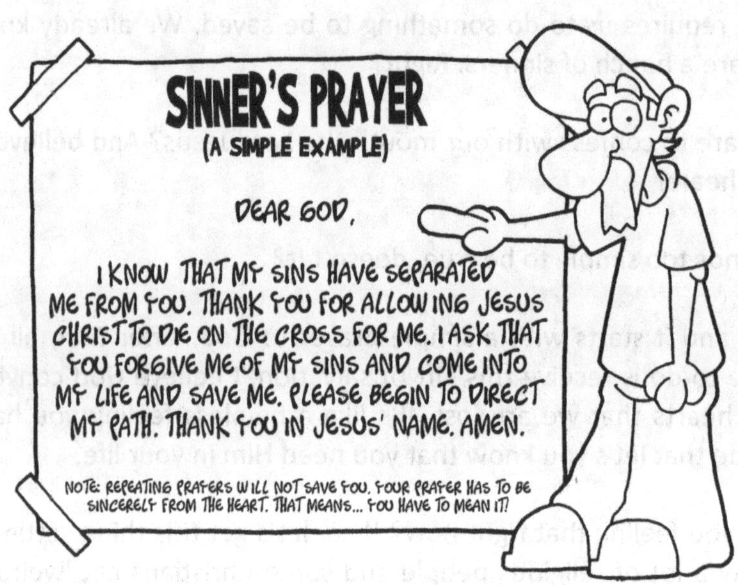

That was easy, wasn't it? Now, I know sparks aren't flying around you and choirs of angels aren't floating by with harps. But, inside you will feel a sense of relief.

It will feel like a ton of bricks have been lifted off your shoulders. Your life may not even show changes immediately, but from this point forward it will. It's like being a new little plant. You will begin growing. That's why they call it being 'born again'. You have a new life! It's up to you make it grow. You can do this by going to church, reading the Bible, and praying every day. Every step in your life from this day on is a 'stepping stone' towards Jesus and growth in your spirituality.

Spiritual Fertilizer

"I'm saved and I know where I'm going when I die. I'm cool with that! But, what should I be doing until then?"

The answer is simple! I should be growing! You should be

growing, too! The day we got saved started a new life in us. This is very similar to growing turnip greens in a garden. This new life started as a small seed planted in the ground. Even as a small seed, it's still a turnip green! But you know as well as I do that a plate full of seeds doesn't taste the same as a big plate of turnip greens. The seeds need to grow first.

To help a turnip green grow, it needs some food. Right? It needs some good soil, refreshing water, and some sunlight. The same is true in our Christian walk. Yes, we could stay content with being a seed. But, wouldn't it be better if we started sprouting? A Christian needs some spiritual fertilizer - some

food for the soul.

God provides us with ways to grow. All we have to do is use what He gives us. The soil He provides us is through the relationship we can have in Him through prayer and walking with Him daily. Every day is an opportunity.

We just need to take advantage of it.

Finding a Bible-believing church and actually going to it is a great starting point for growth. I will be the first to admit that going to church was not in my plans. As a young saved *'whooper-snapper'*, I wasn't really a *'people'* person and I hated getting up early on a Sunday morning to hear a long-winded preacher spitting and slobbering on the whole congregation.

The music in church was awful and would always come from people that really shouldn't have been up front singing to people anyway. I spent my time in the back row socializing with my friends. I was young and didn't know what the whole *'church thing'* was about and what it was for.

Church: The Growth Experience

Now that I am older, I realize that it was for my spiritual growth as a baby Christian.

This process of getting up on a Sunday morning, getting dressed, and going to a building and hanging out with all of these *'weird'* people was intended to help me grow. My job was to listen and learn.

I also realize that my attitude towards it was wrong and sitting on the back row was my first mistake. For a young teenager like me, I should have been on the front row listening. Now that I look back, maybe my life wouldn't have drifted away from God as it did. I'll explain more on this later on in this book.

What is *'going to church'* all about?

A church building is a place where believers gather to worship and praise God. It's just a building and as I

explained earlier, by *'just going'* doesn't save you. Only God can do that! We go there to worship Him and praise Him for who He is – He's God!

It's also a place to *'get your learning on'*. This is accomplished by singing praises, praying, and listening to what the preacher has to say. God uses these tools to teach us stuff from His Word.

> ***O come, let us sing unto the LORD: let us make a joyful noise to the rock of our salvation. – Psalm 95: 1***

Depending on the church, the music is a big part of worship. There are many scriptures throughout the Bible that encourages us to sing songs of praises to God. Actually, the Book of Psalms is simply a book full of song lyrics. It can be in a traditional music style or contemporary music style. It really doesn't matter as long as it's joyful. People will argue about the type of music being played at church and say that only one style is acceptable, but it's not about the style as it is the *'heart'* in which it's worshiped. No one ever taught me this concept about Christian music, but it was in the Bible if I had just taken the time to read it. Plus, when you are singing with right heart, the bad singers start to sound pretty good. Our focus is more on what they are singing instead of how well they sing it. And that's the truth!

A preacher plays a big part in the service because he is a God-called man to deliver the Word. He is the guy that stands in the front of the church with the suit on. If you are in a Baptist church, you will recognize him because he will be the one that speaks the loudest and has the biggest belly. He will be the sweaty man that spits on the congregation sitting on the front row during the services. He is also the first one in line at the *'all you can eat'* buffet dinner restaurant after the church services are over. I'm sorry. I had to throw that in there.

Being a preacher is a big responsibility. The Lord gives him a message to share with the people at church. It is up to him to deliver it. If he delivers something that was not given to him by God, he is going to be in some serious trouble. The preacher has to be very careful in his preaching. He is responsible for what comes out of his mouth.

On the flip side of this, we have to realize that the preacher is just a man. He will make mistakes and is not perfect. Many people will stop going to a particular church or to church, in general, because of something a preacher did that was not acceptable. We should not be followers of preachers, but followers of Jesus Christ. However, we should listen as the Word is being presented to us and follow along with our Bibles open. Listening was another mistake I made earlier in my life.

Preachers ain't perfect! They're human just like we are!

Prayer: For More Growth

Praying is our way of communicating with God. Just like with all types of relationships, good communication is the way to make it stronger. That's why

a lot of marriages don't work out. Many times it's because one person does all the talking, or no one is listening, or that nobody talks or listens at all. It just doesn't work!

Prayer keeps our spiritual life alive! Don't you want to live? Get your prayer on!

By praying to God, we can ask for forgiveness of our sins. We can tell Him how our day is going and let Him know the areas we need help. We can ask for things in our life and even pray for other people's needs. It's like talking to a good friend or better yet, we are talking directly to our Father in Heaven. It helps us to grow spiritually, especially when we see the things we pray for come to pass.

Praying is done in church. It can be done as a group or you can pray as an individual at the altar or right where you sit. But, it's not the only place! You can pray anytime and anywhere. You can pray at home, at somebody else's home, or even on aisle 3 at your local Wally World. It doesn't matter as long as you pray! Most importantly, pray daily!

Bible: The Growth Continues

There's a book that sits around in many homes all over the world.

It's usually the one that's tucked away with dust covering it. It's called the Bible. Even though many people own it, it's rare that people actually read it! For a Christian, it's like an instruction manual for living. It's food for the soul. Its God's words in book form so that we can grow spiritually.

The problem is that many people see it is as just a book with words; like a hard to read novel. It's full of 'thee's' and 'thou's' and it's hard to understand. It has stories in there that really don't apply to us, right? Wrong!

Living the Christian life requires reading the instruction manual.

Have you ever tried to put something together or use something without the manual? There were always parts left over or it didn't work the way it's supposed to. Right?

The same is true in our Christian walk. If you try it without the manual, you'll end up face down in the middle of the road. I know from experience, but I am thankful that Jesus was there to pick me up!

There is so much stuff written in the pages of the Bible. It covers everything! Any topic you want to know about, it's in there! There's anything from basic life principles to the history of man. It does include stories of people and their experiences. Why? The purpose is so that we can use their life of accomplishments or mistakes to help make ours better. We can learn from them. It's so cool! The more you put into it, the more you will get out of it.

To sum it all up, basic spiritual growth begins with going to church, prayer and reading the Bible. You can only grow from here!

The Battle Is On! Like A Chicken Bone

Just when you thought that being a Christian was easy, bad things come into your life. Troubles seem to come at you like darts flying at you from everywhere. It may seem like you are now being tempted with things from your past. You may be tempted with things that affect your weaknesses. It's all part of the plan.

It's a battle and we have an enemy! Satan is his name. You may have heard of him. Don't be '*skeered*'! He's not that cute little cartoon you see on television and he's not that scary demon you see in the horror movies. According to the Bible, he is an angel – a fallen angel. He was with God before the world began. He has been trying to mess things up from the day that God created Adam and Eve.

Remember hearing about Adam and Eve?

In the first few chapters of Genesis, you'll read where Satan tempted them into eating the forbidden fruit. By doing so, sin began and it has been growing ever since. He is in the world today along with his band of devils trying to trip people up. He tries to prevent people from getting saved and makes life hard for the average Christian. The purpose in all of this is to mess up God's work in this world and in His work in the people that live in it.

Keep this in mind, God is creating and preparing a place for His people. Folks, this world that we currently live in is not our home! He is returning one day to take his people to their real home. Who gets to go? It's the people that have been saved. That is why Satan works so hard. His days are numbered and he already knows where he's going and it's not good. His purpose is to take people with him - the lost and unsaved. Did you get that?

I bet you're thinking...

I'm saved, so why is he messing with me?

That's an easy question to answer. You could be the link to someone else getting saved. Your witness and testimony could be what leads them to a relationship with the Lord. You will notice that he works on you the hardest when you are trying to live right. If you are living sinfully, Satan doesn't have to do much to you. You have already lost your witnessing ability. What else does he need to do? He's got you right where he wants you - **DEFEATED**.

But, as you grow in the Lord, you are gaining strength and will be used to reach others. Satan hates this idea and will start throwing the darts. He wants you dead and out of the picture! You have become a hindrance to his master minded plans. Watch out!

That's why it is so important to apply

the *'spiritual fertilizer'* to your life - church, prayer, and Bible. When you are following Jesus, you will be able to recognize Satan's devilish schemes against you.

> ***There hath no temptation taken you but such as is common to man: but God is faithful, who will not suffer you to be tempted above that ye are able; but will with the temptation also make a way to escape, that ye may be able to bear it. – 1 Corinthians 10: 13***

Here's where it gets tricky. As a child of God, He is watching over you. There is nothing that Satan does to you that God doesn't know about. As mean as it may sound, God allows Satan to tempt you. Yep! That's right! We can learn this from the Book of Job. This doesn't make God bad! It is part of His way of strengthening you as a Christian.

However, He will never let you be tempted more than you can bear without His help!

Temptations are coming. What are they? These will be the things that come into your life that make you think,

"Hmm...Should I or shouldn't I?"

This could be almost anything. Temptations come from Satan and are directed by God. As we discussed earlier, temptations will either make us stronger or they will defeat us if we agree to give in to them.

You can almost know what your temptations will be by knowing what your weaknesses are. If the Lord rescued you from abusing drugs and alcohol, you can be guaranteed that these will come back into your life in the form of a temptation. The temptation in itself is not wrong, it's when you give into them that it becomes a sin. Are you hearing me?

Many people suffer from spiritual depression because they don't know why they are being tempted with these things that may have destroyed them in the past. They think it's their fault and feel like they have been defeated. Here's your wake up call! It's just a

temptation! That's all! Rebuke it and send it back to Satan from where it came! Keep moving on and get over it! Don't let it get you down! If you're down and out because of it, then Satan has won the battle anyway.

Once again, temptations come from Satan. Always remember that! It's important to know.

Submit yourselves therefore to God. Resist the devil, and he will flee from you. — James 4: 7

Trials, on the other hand, are a different story. What are trials? I'll try to explain. Trials, sometimes called *'valleys'*, enter our lives from time to time. They usually appear when things seem to be going great.

They can almost be like a messed up deer hunting trip. You deer hunters will be able to relate to this. You are wearing your camouflage sitting up in a deer stand. Everything is going great! You have your gun ready and deer are everywhere! It's going to be a great hunting day! All of a sudden it starts to rain! The deer scatter and you have to climb down from the tree soaking wet. Your legs start chaffing as you walk the long trail back to our 4 x 4 pick up truck. You are feeling miserable and you weren't able to get a deer.

Why did this have to happen? Why do you have to go through this?

You call your friend, Bob, on your outdated cell phone telling him what you just went through as you drive back home disgusted with the way the day ended. You are going through all kinds of emotions. You are mad, sad and everything else other than glad. You know what I'm saying?

The next day, you try hunting again. Before you leave, you check the weather report on the news to see if it will rain. The weatherman says, *"It will be sunny all day!"* You bring an umbrella and an extra pair of socks anyway – just in case. This time you pull your trailer carrying your ATV (All Terrain Vehicle) that you got for Christmas last year with you in case of an emergency. Now you are prepared and learned a lesson!

The purpose of this long drawn out story is to say that God is ultimately in control and allows trials to happen in your life to make you stronger. There is something about them that help you develop character. They make you better prepared for future

trials and you are able to use the experience to teach others and help them. Remember Bob from the story? Guess what? He doesn't go deer hunting anymore without bringing an extra pair of socks because he learned something from your experience, too. Pretty cool, huh?

Just like temptations, trials seem to focus on your weak areas in your walk with Jesus.

Suppose you have a love for money and material things. Guess what your trial will be? Yep, you guessed it! Money issues! It could happen in the form of losing your job or down time in your business. Who knows? But, the important things you will learn from it are to trust God with all of your heart, He is your provider – NOT YOU, and to be content with what you have. I know this one from personal experience.

What if you have anger issues? Guess what your trial will be? You will be hit with things in order to make you mad. You will eventually learn to control your temper and thank God for working with you.

The victories come when we *'pass the tests'*. When you are tempted and you are able to push it away, you have just won a victory. Congratulations!

When you are in a trial and you make it through praising God, you have just won a victory. You are on a roll! Now take a look at yourself. You are stronger, better, and more usable to God to win others to Him. It's all part of the process and you're in it! Why would God go through all of this trouble for you?

That's an easy one. He loves you!

The final victory comes when Jesus returns to take us home to be with Him. What an awesome day that will be! Now that you know the basics of being a Christian and what it's all about, it's time to *'walk the walk'*. This means *'being a light in the world'* and sharing what you know about

Jesus. I would be lying to you if I said it was easy. It's not! The temptations and the fact that we are all just too lazy prevent us from doing everything the Lord requires us to do.

Walkin' the Walk

There are a lot of people out there that will say that they are a Christian. It's not up to us to decide if they are speaking the truth. This is up to them and their relationship with God. But, I believe if we are going to say we are a Christian, we need to show it in the way we live our lives. We need to *'walk the walk'*.

As a child of God, our life should show a change. That means we shouldn't be doing the old sinful things we used to do. This life should reflect Jesus. Have you heard the old saying, *"What would Jesus do?"*? This question could be applied to every choice we have to make.

I also know that we aren't perfect. We are going to make mistakes. But, we shouldn't let that way of thinking prevent us from trying. We should strive to be like Jesus every day.

Here's an example:

What if the tire company, **Not Good Enough Year**, thought the same way. What if they thought, "Well, I know I'm supposed to make good tires and that people out there depend on me to provide them, but I'm not perfect. So, I'll just sit here and sorta throw something together and see what happens."

I imagine a lot of people driving cars and trucks will be affected by it. Some will end up in ditches and may never get to their destination. You see where I'm going with this? It's about making the effort to do the best you can. People's lives are at stake!

'Off' With The Old And 'On' With The New

Before you were saved, you may have been in a lifestyle that you know Jesus wouldn't approve of. This could be almost anything. I won't sit here and list the many things that could fall in this category because you know the ones that pertain to you. These made up the 'old' self of your sinful nature.

Now, here's the problem. You are saved and still doing the *'old'* things that you used to do. Your *'new'* life doesn't reflect a change. You are not living by what you read in the Bible or what you are being taught at church, but by your sinful nature. It could be that you are not reading the Bible or going to church at all and are just *'winging'* your new Christian walk. It's not going to work!

This creates a bad situation in your relationship with Jesus and to others around

you. You are missing out on the spiritual joy of being saved. You are basically the 'old' you with a Jesus label. This is good if all you want is a free ticket to Eternity. But that's not what being a Christian is about. God has a purpose for you and will use you, if you let Him, to reach out to others. That's when *'being saved'* gets exciting and has a greater meaning in your life. Allow Him to change you!

The Suit And Tie Christian

Before I start on this topic, let me tell you that wearing a suit and tie is not a bad thing. Actually, Christians that wear suits and ties look good and I mean that. That is the main purpose of saying it: Christians that just *'look'* good. A person could be sinfully rotten to the core, but when they put a suit and tie on, they fit in with the rest of the Christians in church on Sunday morning.

Being a Christian is a spiritual thing - it's what's on the inside that counts. It's a relationship with Jesus Christ that goes straight to the heart. When this kind of relationship goes to the heart, it will begin to manifest itself outwards in our actions and in our words. Are you with me?

Many people are deceived by the *'suit and tie'* Christian because they only *'look'* good. If you were to spend some time with them, you would realize what is really going on in their heart. You could see it in their actions in the way they conduct their life. When they speak, their words coming out would make you think differently of them.

Knowing that, it is important to realize that *'walking the walk'* is more than just trying to look good. It's about *'looking good'* because of the relationship we have in Jesus and what He has placed in our heart.

Holier Than Thou Christian

I have met some Christian people that are quick to judge people. Being a Christian myself, these people were quick to tell me everything that I was doing wrong. This made me want to quit going to church and socializing with the *'Christian'* people. I later learned that this type of judging is OK when you are trying to help someone and are doing it in a loving way. This should also be followed by a solution to their problem.

Pride is a killer, folks! People can easily fill themselves with the pride of being a Christian and the spiritual things they know that not only do they kill their witnessing abilities but they actually kill the chances of bringing others to Jesus. They can also kill the growth of other Christians. It's a bad deal! Jesus wasn't about all that!

If you read the Bible and learn how Jesus

was, you'll learn that He never had this type of attitude toward others. He had compassion for His followers in teaching them how they should and shouldn't be and He had compassion for the ones that didn't know Him. By His example is why people chose to follow Him. He would socialize with the sinners and lead them by being the example. He didn't walk around with a stick bopping people on the hands every time they did something wrong. If He did see something wrong in a person's life, He would lovingly tell them and provide a solution. This is how we should be.

It's great to be a Christian and to have grown spiritually in our walk. But we need to understand that without God's mercy on our life and His spiritual guidance, we are nothing more than a sinner ourselves. When we meet people that are lost, we need to focus on the sin in their lives and not on that person.

And remember God loves them, too.

It's Not Just About Us
It's About Others

The day we became saved, God could have just taken us home to be with Him. We're saved! What other reason would we need to be here on Earth? Since we don't belong here anymore, we may as well just move on to Glory Land. So, why are we still here?

Listen to this:

Go ye therefore, and teach all nations, baptizing them in the name of the Father, and of the Son, and of the Holy Ghost: Teaching them to observe all things whatsoever I have commanded you: and, lo, I am with you alway, even unto the end of the world. Amen. – Matthew 28: 19, 20

Jesus said it right there. We are called to be His disciples to go out and teach others. A disciple is a follower of Jesus; to follow

His teachings and to be like Him. Just like the twelve disciples in the Bible, we have a mission statement:

"To be a light in the world and to lead others to Jesus by spreading the Gospel and being an example to the world."

Being a Christian means being Christ-like. You may not know this, but being a Christian is not just about you. The world teaches us to be concerned about ourselves and nobody else. What do we want out of life? How can we make our life better? Watch television and you will discover that all of the commercial ads are directed to you.

This is not what Jesus is all about. Your Christian life should reflect the One that saved you. Why is this so important?

Here's the scenario:

- **The world is full of people that don't know Jesus as their Lord and Savior.**
- **Jesus is returning one day to take His children home.**
- **The ones that remain will burn in a lake of fire.**

Who are His children? It's the people that are saved. Does He want everyone to spend Eternity with Him? Yes, He does. Unfortunately, it's this thing called 'sin' that we talked about a few pages back that separates us. He gives us all a *freedom of choice'*. It's a choice to turn from sin, ask for forgiveness and to turn to Him. It's plain and simple! We have a choice!

What is our role as a Christian in all of this? The answer is to lead others to Him. It's about *'being a light in the world'*. We are the link that connects them to a relationship with Jesus. We can't save them, but we can lead them to the One that can. Is this sinking in?

This is why it's so important to truly *'walk the walk'*. It's not so that WE can live a better life, but to show others the *'better life'* we have in Jesus. Think about it!

When you start living the life Jesus wants you to have, people are going to want it, too. If they don't see a change in you, then how will they know Jesus? Time is running short! What are you waiting on? Walk the walk! Be a light!

My Testimony

A testimony is what you have after the Lord saves you or delivers you from something. It's like our story to tell others of what Jesus has done for us. Every Christian will have one. If you are saved today, you have one, too.

Our testimony is what we will use to lead others to Jesus. It is how we are able to witness to other people. Believe it or not, that *'thing'* that Jesus delivered you from is probably what is holding a lot of people you meet back from a relationship with Jesus. It is very interesting how this works. It's like God will put people that are not saved in your life that will need to hear your testimony. The amazing thing is that they are going through the same thing or have been through it and don't know how to deal with it. All of a sudden they meet you; a person with a similar story, but this time there is a solution. His name is Jesus.

I accepted Jesus as my Lord and Savior when I was 14 years old. My father had left me and my mother when I was five and she was forced to raise me on her own. The Lord stepped in during my teenage years because I needed a father in my life. He became my Heavenly Father!

Do you realize what happens to many teenagers growing up without a father? Let's just say that many of them end up going down the wrong roads in life. They wind up in places and situations that they shouldn't be in. God gave me His protection and put me on the path of righteousness as long as I stayed focused in it.

Within that same year, I also met Satan. I didn't really recognize him at first because he disguised himself in the things I allowed in my life. Pornography was his first trick. This is a big temptation for a young kid with raging hormones, but I took the bait. This went on for years and found its way on my computer screen as I got older.

Satan also knew I had a passion for music. I enjoyed listening to it and playing it on the guitar. Its original purpose was intended to glorify and praise God, but wound up on the stages at the local bars playing as a live band.

This introduced a new temptation given by Satan that created an addiction within me that I would later battle with in life. It's the poison called alcohol. It destroys you from the inside out and affects the people around you. Alcohol every day pushes the family away! And that's exactly what it was doing. Because of my addiction, I would be re-creating my life story all over again with my kids. They would be fatherless and the vicious cycle would continue.

That's when Jesus showed up! He woke me up when my son got saved. At that time, my son needed someone to lead him to the Lord and I wasn't able to do it. I should have been, but couldn't. My life was a mess! I had to take him to someone that could. This burned me deep and helped me realize that I needed Jesus back in my life, too. It wasn't that I need to be saved again. It was that I needed to go back to where I left Him. I had turned away.

Years later, the pornography is gone and the alcohol has been traded in for the living water that Jesus freely offers. I have been 'living' since then. This new change has created a great life for me and my family. It has created a ministry that God has used has to reach many people and touch lives. I realize now that this was part of God's original plan before I decided to change it. I am ashamed that it took twenty years to wake me up. This is my testimony. Thank you Jesus!

Once again, the main purpose of this book is to use what the Lord has given me to share with you.

My heart goes out to all Christians everywhere – all over the world. If the lessons I have learned from my life can be used to help someone out there, then that's what I want to do. I'm sure there are Christian people out there like me that don't know what the whole deal is. Some are blinded by Satan on their purpose on this Earth and what they should be doing until the Lord comes back. I hope this book will prevent them from wasting 20 years of their life going in the wrong direction.

If you don't know Jesus as your Lord and Savior, I encourage you to make that step. Being a Christian isn't what the world says it is. It's being what Jesus wants us to be: happy and full of joy. If you need that in your life today, Jesus can and will freely give it to you. All you have to do is ask Him.

If you're a Christian, begin living by His Word and reading it daily. Don't sit around like stagnated water! Do something with the new life God has given you. Reach out to people that need this life, too. Learn more about Jesus. Live the life that He wants you to live. It brings life – life abundantly. Let's do something! You know?

I hope you received what you needed today. And please share this book with someone you know!

More From A BackPew Review

Thanks for reading this guide. We hope you enjoyed it and will continue to read our other guides in the series. Here is a complete list of our books from the series:

- **What Does It Mean To Be A Christian**
- **Acts: The Early Days Of The Christian Church**
- **Being A Dad According To The Bible**
- **The Prison Letters: Apostle Paul's Letters To The Early Church**
- **Exodus: The Journey To The Promised Land**
- **Genesis: The Beginning, The Fall And The Promise**
- **The Seven Letters: The New Testament Letters To The Early Church**
- **The Gospel From A Four-Sided View**
- **Healthy Eating: A Few Tips From The Bible**
- **Being A Man According To The Bible**
- **A Marriage Built To Last: Learn What The Bible Says About Marriage**
- **How Do I Pray? The Bible Tells Us How**
- **Revelation: The End Is Near?**